BATH AND BRISTOL

Copyright © 2017 Read Books Ltd.
This book is copyright and may not be
reproduced or copied in any way without
the express permission of the publisher in writing

British Library Cataloguing-in-Publication Data
A catalogue record for this book is available from the
British Library

BATH & BRISTOL

PAINTED BY
LAURA·A·HAPPERFIELD
DESCRIBED BY
STANLEY·HUTTON

BATH ABBEY. WEST DOOR

PREFACE

Few towns in the British Empire are more historically interesting or possess more picturesque attractions than the twin cities of Bath and Bristol; both situated on the River Avon, and both having their origins in unrecorded history. Yet, whilst the one is a classic example of the grandeur that was Rome, the other has been nourished from its very beginning into its present greatness, by commerce, and commerce alone.

In the following pages it has been the aim of the writer to present to the reader the things that matter which have given Bath and Bristol an imperishable place in our Empire's history, and world-wide fame.

Apart from his own researches the writer acknowledges with gratitude his indebtedness to the works of the late John Taylor, and to Monsieur A. Barbeau's monumental work on Bath.

STANLEY HUTTON.

CONTENTS

CHAP.		PAGE
I.	Bath	1
II.	Bristol	19
III.	Empire Building	23
IV.	Privateering	35
V.	Clifton: Its Beauty and Associations	45
VI.	Churches and their Associations	63
VII.	Bristol's connection with Literature	92
VIII.	Art and the Drama	132
IX.	Science and Religion	150
X.	Charities	166
XI.	The Riots	179
	Index	193

LIST OF ILLUSTRATIONS

BATH

1.	BATH ABBEY, WEST DOOR	*Frontispiece*
2.	THE ROMAN BATH	3
3.	BATH ABBEY, TOMB OF BISHOP MONTAGUE	5
4.	PULTENEY BRIDGE	12
5.	BATH STREET AND MINERAL WATER FOUNTAIN	14
6.	PRIOR PARK	16

Plan of Bath facing p. 18

BRISTOL

7.	CLIFTON COLLEGE	23
8.	THE "SULTANA," A TIMBER SHIP	26
9.	IN LEIGH WOODS	51
10.	SUSPENSION BRIDGE, CLIFTON	62
11.	BRISTOL CATHEDRAL, WEST FRONT	65
12.	THE CLOISTERS, BRISTOL CATHEDRAL	71
13.	ST. MARY REDCLIFFE, LOOKING EAST	74
14.	ST. MARY REDCLIFFE, FROM PRINCE'S WHARF	80
15.	ST. STEPHEN'S CHURCH	83
16.	THE "MENAPIA," AN IRISH TRADER (ST. STEPHEN'S CHURCH IN THE BACKGROUND)	94
17.	BRISTOL BRIDGE	101
18.	AUTUMN AT FRENCHAY	108
19.	MARY-LE-PORT STREET: A BIT OF OLD BRISTOL	161
20.	ST. PETER'S HOSPITAL	176

Plan of Bristol facing p. 192

BATH AND BRISTOL

CHAPTER I

BATH

ENSHRINED in the bosom of the green eternal hills, through which the crystal Avon runs, she lies—Queen of the radiant West country, dowered so richly by nature that, once seen, her charms become an unforgettable memory; fit setting indeed her wondrous amphitheatre of lofty downs for the glorious domestic architecture of the Woods, who found her humble and who made her great. Truly, they ushered in her golden age by their architectural genius, which created the "handsomest houses in the world and the noblest round of domestic edifices in the solar system." Not in England surely, if in the whole modern world, is there to be found a nobler monument of architectural splendour than the Woods have here raised.

There is a charm for English eyes in the tender browns and greys of the old stone-built city, and when we turn from the man-made to the God-made—when we allow our gaze to mount upward by way of the climbing terraces of Lansdown, and thence to sweep the whole environment of Bath—the unequalled beauty of our

Bath and Bristol

English rural scenery is once more brought home to us. Downward from the foot of the spectator descend sloping meadows of the lovely glen between Widcombe and Prior Park, the site of a "God's Acre" as peaceful as its sequestered dead; over against him to the north rise the wooded heights of Lansdown, its summit crowned by Beckford's Tower; from the eastward the Avon steals like a silver serpent through the fringing willows of its valley; whilst tier upon tier the undulations of the hills fade fainter and fainter in the haze of "that broad water of the West"—the Bristol Channel.

Well might Swinburne's muse pay eloquent tribute to her all-compelling charm in his "Ballad of Bath"—

> "Like a queen enchanted who may not laugh or weep,
> Glad at heart and guarded from change and care like ours,
> Girt about with beauty by days and nights that creep,
> Soft as breathless ripples that softly shoreward sweep,
> Lies the lovely city whose grace no grief deflowers.
> Age and grey forgetfulness, Time that shifts and veers,
> Touch not thee, our fairest, whose charm no rival nears.
> Hailed as England's Florence of one whose praise gives grace,
> Landor, once thy lover, a name that love reveres:
> Dawn and noon and sunset are one before thy face."

To see this noble city at its best it should be seen in early summer from the vantage-point of Beechen cliff, from which a magnificent panoramic view is obtainable. How much Bath's architectural beauty is due to its geologic formation is proved to demonstration from the fact that nearly all its buildings are constructed of the native stone quarried in the neighbourhood and so well known all over the world by the appellation of "Bath

THE ROMAN BATH

Bath

stone." To the initiative of Ralph Allen, the man of Bath, is the credit due of utilizing the admirable building material and introducing it to the notice of the Woods, by whom it was first used in the construction of Allen's splendid mansion, Prior Park.

Apart from the impressive dignity of its domestic architecture, alike in unity and harmoniousness of design, the chief glories of Bath are its unique Roman baths, whose waters have flowed on from time undated, and its beautiful Abbey Church, fitly termed the Lantern of the West.

Undoubtedly the Roman baths are among the most striking antiquities of the Latin race in Western Europe. There can be no question that Bath's celebrity from the earliest times was due to her thermal springs, which were probably first utilized by the Romans in the reign of Claudius, when south and west Britain were subjugated to Roman rule (A.D. 49).

These magnificently constructed baths are a triumphal proof of the architectural and building skill of the Romans two thousand years ago, for they are of the best age of Roman workmanship. Owing to the number of altars which have been found in the city dedicated to the Goddess Sul or Sul-Minerva, it has been assumed that its name was originally "Aquæ Sulis," or the waters of the sun. Direct proof, however, of this assumption has not yet been obtained. The well-known legend re Bladud having been driven from his father's court as a leper, falling so low as to follow the employment of a swineherd and infecting the swine with the disease, and these wallowing in the mire impregnated by the hot

Bath and Bristol

springs recovered; thereupon the prince bathed in the waters and was healed of his leprosy, is doubtless a charming but idle fiction. Yet that the fame of the waters was well established in the Middle Ages is abundantly clear by the panegyric of the author of the *Gesta Stephani*, who, writing in the first half of the twelfth century, says—

"There is a city distant six [*sic*] miles from Bristol, where, through hidden channels, are thrown up streamlets of water, warmed without human agency, and from the very bowels of the earth, into a receptacle beautifully constructed with chamber arches. These form baths in the middle of the city, warm and wholesome, and charming to the eye. . . . Sick persons from all England resort thither to bathe in these healing waters, and the strong also, to see these wonderful burstings-out of warm water and to bathe in them."

Many evidences of Roman occupation have been found in and around the city; a large number of these have fortunately found a permanent home in the Bath Literary and Scientific Institution. Among them is a colossal female head, found in 1714. The figure to which it belonged probably stood eight feet high. The head-dress is covered with small curls, and is authoritatively considered to be about the time of Agricola or Titus.

Situated in the heart of Bath and adjacent to its famous baths stands its Abbey Church, dedicated to St. Peter and St. Paul. Originally founded as a nunnery by Osric, 676, it was destroyed by Danish marauders and subsequently refounded as a college of secular canons

BATH ABBEY, TOMB OF BISHOP MONTAGUE

Bath

by Offa, *circa* 775. Two centuries later it passed into the possession of the Benedictines. Finally the celebrated John de Villula bought it, as well as the whole of the city, for the sum of 500 pounds of silver, and rebuilt it and made it the See of the bishopric instead of Wells, in 1090. This arbitrary proceeding occasioned endless disputes between the monastic body of the Abbey and the canons of Wells, and at length the matter was somewhat adjusted by his successor, who decided that henceforth the bishop should bear the joint title of Bath and Wells, and be elected by an equal number of each city's representatives.

At the great despoliation in Henry the Eighth's reign, dark days descended on the Abbey, and on the city's refusal to purchase it for 500 marks, it was stripped of all its stained glass, lead, etc., and the " bare carcase " sold to Humphrey Colles in 1542, who again disposed of it to Matthew Colthurst, and his heir ultimately gave it to the city, in whose possession it has remained ever since. During the nineteenth century, through the splendid generosity and initiative of a former rector of Bath, a great scheme of restoration, extending over many years, was successfully carried out under the direction of that eminent architect, Sir Gilbert Scott. It will be noticed that the west front is particularly striking, with its magnificent window of seven lights flanked by turrets, on which are carved angels ascending and descending by means of ladders, to commemorate a vision of Bishop King in 1499.

The interior well deserves quaint old Fuller's praise as being both " spacious and specious, the most lightsome as ever I beheld " ; thus the number and size of its windows,

Bath and Bristol

largely filled with stained glass, fully justifies its proud title of "the Lantern of the West." Its great walls are crowded with monumental tributes to the departed, many of them chaste, beautiful, and interesting. So numerous indeed are these mural tablets that there is truth as well as wit expressed in Dr. Harington's epigrammatic lines—

> "These walls, adorned with monument and bust,
> Show how Bath waters serve to lay the dust."

Among those entombed within its walls is James Quin, the famous actor and contemporary of Garrick, who wrote his epitaph, which runs as follows :—

> "That tongue which set the table on a roar,
> And charmed the publick ear, is heard no more;
> Closed are those eyes, the harbingers of wit,
> Which spake before the tongue, what Shakespeare writ;
> Cold is the hand which, living, was stretched forth,
> At friendship's call, to succour modest worth.
> Here lies James Quin! deign reader to be taught,
> Whate'er thy strength of body, force of thought,
> In Nature's happiest mould however cast,
> 'To this complexion thou must come at last.'"

There is, too, a quaint old-world charm in the lines to the memory of Lady Jane Waller; but the epitaph that always arrests attention is that written by the famous poet Dryden to Mary Frampton, which commences—

> "Below this marble monument is laid
> All that Heaven wants of this celestial mayd:
> Preserve, O sacred tomb, thy trust consigned!
> The mould was made on purpose for the mind. . . ."

Bath

There, too, is interred Malthus, of population fame, and Beau Nash. In the south aisle will be found the monument erected by the Corporation to the latter's memory.

Great, however, as are Bath's architectural claims to distinction, which have made her one of the most stately cities in Europe, she has, too, a wondrous roll-call of famous men and women who have added lustre to her annals in her golden period of the eighteenth century. Her streets, indeed, to-day are haunted with illustrious memories of the unforgettable statesmen, poets, actors, wits, and authors who once yielded homage by their presence to her healing waters and delightful situation on the banks of the Avon.

And he who thus made Bath the Mecca of England, if not of the Continent, was Richard Nash, the uncrowned King of Bath, who, born of respectable parentage at Swansea, entered the army, sold out, and became a law student. Subsequently a love of pleasure took him to Bath, where he soon attracted attention, and the Master of Ceremonies dying soon after, Nash was elected to the position, in which he revealed remarkable social talents. Without necessarily purging her of her vices and follies, he most certainly refined and kept them within the bounds of decency and order, and in course of time his power so increased that he was enabled to formulate a code of social rules of etiquette governing Bath's amusements. And what is more, absolute power was vested in him to prevent their infringement, whether by inadvertence or design. How socially all-powerful he was is proved in the case of the Duchess of Queensberry having, on one occasion, come to a dance wearing a white apron, which he had forbidden; thereupon he tore it off and threw it away, saying that such articles of attire were only suitable for servants.

The thing was done with such an air that the good-natured Duchess accepted his reproof, and with great good sense and humour apologized to His Majesty. So highly was he esteemed that in 1738 he was the recipient of a gold snuff-box from the Prince of Wales, in addition to numerous presents from the nobility, and a full-length portrait of him was placed in the Assembly Rooms between the busts of Newton and Pope, which occasioned the following witty epigram:—

> "The picture placed the busts between
> Gives satire its full strength,
> Wisdom and wit are little seen,
> But folly at full length."

Nash died in 1761 at the age of eighty-seven, and the city which had neglected him in his old age made tardy amends by giving him a splendid funeral.

The popular opinion of this remarkable arbiter of fashion is happily hit off in Anstey's famous "New Bath Guide"—

> "Long reigned the great Nash, this omnipotent Lord,
> Respected by youth and by parents adored,
> For him not enough at a ball to preside,
> Th' unwary and beautiful nymph would he guide;
> Oft tell her the tale, how the credulous maid
> By man, by perfidious man, is betrayed;
> Taught Charity's hand to relieve the distrest,
> While tears have his tender compassion expressed:
> But, alas! he is gone, and the city can tell
> How in years and in glory lamented he fell. . . ."

Bath

Far nobler, however, was the personality of the man of Bath—Ralph Allen of Prior Park, whose goodness is immortalized in Pope's couplet—

"Let humble Allen, with an awkward shame,
 Do good by stealth and blush to find it fame."

This famous postal pioneer, who conferred by his cross-posts system so great a benefit on his country, and thereby amassed much wealth, was to a large extent, through the architectural genius of the Woods, the creator of eighteenth-century Bath. In Richardson's continuation of Defoe's *Tour of Great Britain*, he mentions that "the stoneyard of this great and good man, who might be styled the genius of Bath, is on the banks of the Avon. In it is wrought the freestone dug from the quarries in Combe Down."

At his hospitable table this princely benefactor to Bath was wont to entertain men of the highest rank and talent. Among these may be named the elder Pitt, Fielding, Richardson, and Pope. Fielding, to whom Allen, whilst personally unknown to him, generously sent £200, is thought to have drawn him to the life as Squire Allworthy in *Tom Jones*; in any case, Fielding has put on record his warm admiration and gratitude by dedicating *Amelia* to Ralph Allen.

Pope, before his rupture with Allen on account of Martha Blount, esteemed him highly. It is a proof of the waspish nature of the poet that he bequeathed £200 to Ralph Allen to wipe out the obligation he was under to his quondam friend's generosity.

Tradition avers that when Pope's executors paid over the legacy to Allen, he remarked, that if Mr. Pope

Bath and Bristol

intended it as *compensation* and not as a *compliment*, he should have added another cypher!

The author of the famous satire in verse—the "New Bath Guide"—Christopher Anstey, whose mordant wit was to shoot folly as it flies, must not be forgotten. Alluding to that work in one of his letters, Horace Walpole says: "What pleasure have you to come! There is a new thing published . . . called the 'Bath Guide.' It stole into the world, and for a fortnight no soul looked into it, concluding its name was its true name. No such thing. It is a set of verses, in all kinds of verses, describing the life of Bath, and, incidentally, everything else; but so much wit, so much humour, fun, and poetry, so much originality, never met together before. . . . I can say it by heart though in quarto."

The chief character in the "Guide" is a certain Simkin Blunderhead, through whom Anstey has a shrewd thrust at the Bath doctors, as follows:—

"Since the day that King Bladud first found out the bogs,
And thought them so good for himself and his hogs,
Not one of the faculty ever has tried
Those excellent waters to cure his own hide."

Whilst keenly satirizing the vices and follies of that eighteenth-century Bath, Anstey was equally alive to its delightful situation and amenities, as illustrated herewith—

"Of all the gay places the world can afford,
By gentle and simple for pastime adored,
Fine balls and fine concerts, fine buildings and springs,
Fine walks and fine views, and a thousand fine things,
Not to mention the sweet situation and air;
What place, my dear mother, with Bath can compare?"

Bath

So popular became this " New Bath Guide " that editions succeeded each other with startling rapidity, and when Dodsley the publisher generously restored the copyright to its author after the tenth edition, he frankly confessed that no work he had published had ever brought him in so much money in so short a time.

A City of Memories

To the intelligent stranger versed in England's history and literature, a day's saunter through the city of Bath is nothing short of a revelation, street after street having within its confines homes of departed greatness, the very portals of which are fragrant with golden memories which have become the glorious heritage of present-day Bath : Burke, Pitt, Nelson, Wolfe, Napier, Fielding, Sheridan, Goldsmith, Johnson, Landor, Dickens, and Herschel—to name but a few of those who have immortalized classic Bath.

Both Southey and Landor have placed on record their admiration of this Florence of England. The former, writing to Landor on one occasion, remarks : " Will this find you in the Vale of Ewyas, or have you taken wing to Bath, which, in spite of thirty years' labour toward spoiling it, still remains the pleasantest city in the kingdom ? " Landor in his reply said : " You remind me of Bath ; the South Parade was always my residence in winter ; towards the spring I removed into Pulteney Street —or rather towards summer ; for there were formerly as many nightingales in the garden, and along the river opposite the South Parade, as ever there were in the

Bath and Bristol

bowers of Sahiraz. The situation is unparalleled in beauty, and is surely the warmest in England."

Here Fielding and Smollett found in the Pump Room and the Assembly Rooms the prototypes of their characters delineated in *Tom Jones*, *Amelia*, *Humphry Clinker*, and *Roderick Random*. Smollett was extremely well acquainted with Bath, for, in addition to his novels dealing with its social life, he wrote also an essay on the properties of its waters. Readers of *Roderick Random* will remember that in Chapter LV. the King of Bath has a considerable set back, for the hero's companion, a young lady slightly deformed, on arriving at the Assembly Rooms, is ridiculed by the visitors, which emboldens Nash to further mortify her by asking in a loud voice, as he welcomes her with exaggerated politeness, if she could inform him of the name of Tobit's dog. To which with spirit she replied, " His name was Nash, and an impudent dog he was." This repartee, so richly deserved, quite discomfited " His Majesty."

In *Humphry Clinker* Smollett gives us a picture of taking the Bath waters in his day, for Miss Lydia Melford, the heroine, says—

" At eight in the morning we go in deshabille to the Pump Room, which is crowded like a Welsh fair; and there you see the highest quality and the lowest tradesfolk jostling each other without ceremony—hail, fellow, well met. The noise of the music playing in the gallery, the heat and flavour of such a crowd, and the hum and buzz of their conversation, gave me the headache and vertigo the first day; but afterwards all these things became familiar, and even agreeable. Right under the

PULTENEY BRIDGE

Bath

Pump Room windows is the King's Bath—a huge cistern, where you see the patients sitting up to their necks in hot water. The ladies wear jackets and petticoats of brown linen, with chip hats, in which they fix their handkerchiefs to wipe the sweat from their faces ; but truly, whether it is owing to the steam that surrounds them, or the heat of the water, or the nature of the dress, or all these things together, they looked so flushed and so frightful that I always turn my eyes another way."

Much local colouring will be found in Jane Austen's novels, particularly in *Northanger Abbey* and *Persuasion*. In Fanny Burney's erstwhile famous novel, *Evelina*, readers will find Bath has much prominence. Not only so, but Dickens has immortalized the Queen City of the West in his masterpiece, *Pickwick Papers*; the very title of which has its origin in a Bath innkeeper named Moses Pickwick. And coming down to quite recent date, Mrs. Marshall has given us *Her Season in Bath* ; Egerton and Agnes Castle, *The Bath Comedy* ; and Booth Tarkington, *Monsieur Beaucaire*.

Wandering about this city of deathless memories, we alight on the residence of him who legislated not for a day but for all time—Edmund Burke—the greatest man since Milton, Lord Morley has asserted. And who will be bold enough to deny it ? Not Bath surely, seeing that he found his wife there, and to which he came habitually for rest and enjoyment, and where on the North Parade he spent the last few months of his stricken life. His last letter from thence contains the following touching passage :—

"I have been to Bath these four months for no

Bath and Bristol

purpose, and am therefore to be removed to my own house at Beaconsfield to-morrow, to be nearer a habitation more permanent, humbly and fearfully hoping that my better part may find a better mansion."

Take him for all in all, Bath will not look upon his like again. Well might his friend Goldsmith say of this sublime genius in his " Retaliation "—

"Who, born for a Universe, narrowed his mind,
And to Party gave up what was meant for mankind."

It was in this same house (No. 11) Goldsmith stayed with his friend Lord Clare on his frequent visits to Bath. Their mutual friend, Dr. Samuel Johnson, came on a visit to the city in 1776 to be near his friends the Thrales, where he lodged at The Pelican, since rechristened The Three Cups, in Walcot Street.

Nor must we forget that their brilliant contemporary and friend, Richard Brinsley Sheridan, orator, dramatist, and wit, was most closely associated with Bath, for the romance of his attachment to the lovely Elizabeth Linley is one of the imperishable stories of its past. Apart from being the possessor of a wonderful voice and exquisite beauty, she exerted a magnetic sway over those with whom she came into contact. Fanny Burney records in her famous *Diary* of being absolutely charmed with her. Reynolds and Gainsborough have immortalized her on their glowing canvases. It was to avenge the aspersions on her fair fame that Sheridan had the duel on King's Down with her traducer Mathews. It is, of course, believed by all true Bathonians that their city was the birthplace of Sheridan's dramatic masterpiece, *The Rivals*.

BATH STREET AND MINERAL WATER FOUNTAIN

Bath

Bath is linked, too, with the poets Wordsworth and Southey, the residences of whom have this year been marked with tablets, namely, 9 North Parade and 8 Westgate Buildings.

To the healing springs of Bath came the elder and younger Pitt, the famous statesmen. Pitt, Earl of Chatham, took up his residence at 7 The Circus, which had been expressly built for him, and derived great benefit from the waters. The Great Commoner twice represented Bath in Parliament and was presented with her freedomship. When in 1802 the younger Pitt, worn and harassed with the cares and responsibilities of office, came once more to try the effect of her healing springs, Bathonians could scarcely credit that the quiet, unobtrusive, dignified old gentleman was the great Mr. Pitt—"the Pilot who weathered the storm"—the all-powerful Minister of State.

So great was the esteem in which Pitt was held by the citizens of Bath, that his resignation was looked upon as a public calamity. It was whilst residing at Bath that the news of the battle of Austerlitz reached him and gave him his death-blow.

At Bath came to reside his contemporary, William Beckford—"the Sultan of Lansdown Tower." This princely and eccentric recluse, having vainly desired to acquire Prior Park, bought houses and land at Lansdown, and on its barren slopes he planted innumerable trees. Later he exclaimed, with pardonable pride, "I have crowned Lansdown with a forest." On the summit of that lofty Down, which stands 800 feet above sea-level, he erected the tower known to-day as Beckford's, the height of which is 130 feet. From that lofty point of

Bath and Bristol

vantage Beckford was wont to view his beautiful surroundings. In 1829, being at variance with the Bath authorities over rights of way across his estate there, he wrote his agent as follows :—

" I beg you will inform Mr. Taylor that if I continue to be annoyed with complaints about paths, l shall have to recourse to a sweeping remedy. I shall quit Bath, and immediately upon my departure all my fences upon Lansdown shall be removed, the whole thrown open, and a town of not less than 1500 hovels erected upon the freehold behind my present habitation. It shall be said of me—
'Deposuit potenter de sede et exaltavit humiles.'"

Possessed of enormous wealth, derived from his father, the famous Lord Mayor of London, great social and intellectual advantages, what a barren and wasted life was his. Yet one bequest he has left posterity, his famous and classic Oriental romance, *Vathek*, a proof indeed of extraordinary literary and imaginative power. At his death in 1844 he was interred first in the Abbey precincts, but his remains were subsequently reinterred under the shadow of his own tower at Lansdown.

A street of famous memories is that of Pierrepont, for there lived the celebrated Earl of Chesterfield, the author of the *Letters* to his son, and the recipient of Johnson's scathing epistle. At No. 5 resided that nest of nightingales, the Linleys, where Sheridan's lovely wife was born. There, too, the father of Maria Edgeworth first saw the light. Last, but not least, at No. 2 lived the greatest sailor since the world began—Nelson. In 1797 Bath conferred upon him the freedomship of her

PRIOR PARK

Bath

city, thus honouring alike herself and the future hero of Trafalgar; the mention of whom reminds us that the gallant Sir Sidney Smith spent his boyhood in Bath, and was educated at her grammar school. His master in after years boasted that he had flogged the man who flogged the French, which association is commemorated in its school song—

> "For here, dauntless Sidney, famed heroes among,
> First dreamt of the laurels he gained at Toulon."

Nor must we forget that at No. 5 Trim Street resided the deathless hero of Quebec, General Wolfe, who died gloriously, like Nelson, in the arms of victory.

At 19 Green Park resided for many years the famous military historian, Sir William Napier—one of a band of noble brothers, sons of the beautiful Lady Sarah Lennox, who might have been Queen of England by marrying George III. Sir Joshua Reynolds has given to later generations the portrait of this lovely and remarkable woman.

Here, at Bath, the wizard of the North, Sir Walter Scott, stayed with his uncle, when a boy, at No. 6 South Parade, and whilst on his visit was taken for the first time to a theatre, an event in his life that he graphically recorded. Putting aside the native artists of the city, the Barkers and Beach, Bath's art associations are represented by the world-famous names of Gainsborough and Lawrence. Some of the former's greatest works were here painted, for he spent nearly twenty years of his life in Bath at various addresses; among others, at 14 Abbey Churchyard and 24 The Circus. Apart from his

Bath and Bristol

exquisite landscapes, he painted here many of his masterpieces of portraiture, including Mrs. Sheridan, Burke, Sterne, and above all, his *magnus opus*, the Parish Clerk of Bradford, now one of the glories of the National Gallery. It was at 2 Alfred Street Sir Thomas Lawrence lived when starting out on his brilliantly successful career. Turning from art to science, did not the immortal astronomer, Sir John Herschel, the discoverer of the planet Uranus, spend sixteen years of his life at Bath as a music-master and organist ? Here his most interesting astronomical discoveries were made. In the great field of Arctic exploration, a niche in the temple of fame must be reserved for that intrepid son of Bath, Sir Edward Parry. Bath, too, is the birthplace of the ever-memorable John Hales, and the tireless and voluminous seventeenth-century pamphleteer, William Prynne.

Yet long as this list is of priceless personal associations which enrich and glorify Bath's annals, it could be extended ; but we must forbear to weary the reader, though it can well be understood how strong are its threefold claims upon the attention of visitors—its natural loveliness, its architectural splendour, and its wealth of famous men and women associated with this city of a wondrous past—the Florence of England acclaimed by the poets.

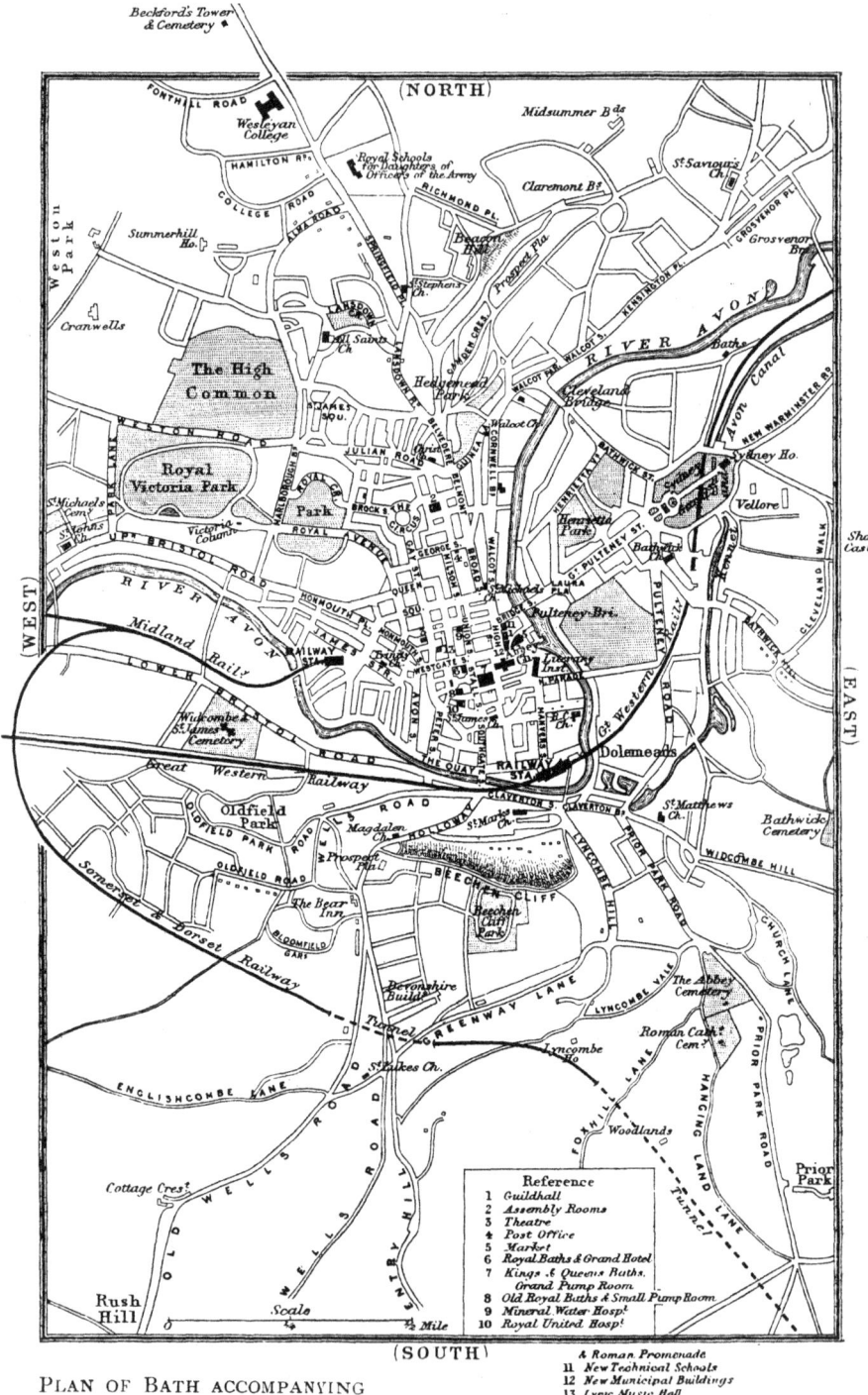

PLAN OF BATH ACCOMPANYING "BATH AND BRISTOL." BY L. A. HAPPERFIELD AND STANLEY HUTTON. Published by A. & C. Black Ltd., London.

CHAPTER II

BRISTOL

BRISTOL, the magnificent gateway to the West country, with an uninterrupted civic history behind her of nearly seven centuries, has a record of which she is justifiably proud. The stranger within her gates soon yields to the charm of her continental colouring, while her stately towers, her spacious squares, her noble almshouses, and her gull-haunted waterways intersecting the very heart of the city, are overwhelming evidence to the intelligent observer that Bristol is indeed no mean city, that behind her is a great and storied past. For hundreds of years she came second only to London in importance. Lord Macaulay in his famous *History* has given her immortal place by his splendid eulogy. Not only so, but in every field of human activity Bristol has carved her name deep and wide in the national life and history. Whether it be in commerce, in art, in science, in literature, in drama, in religion, or philanthrophy, in each and all she has ever been in the foremost files of Time. As early as the first half of the twelfth century she is referred to by William of Malmesbury in his *Chronicle*, when alluding to the Vale of Gloucester, as follows :—

"In this same valley is a very celebrated town by name Bristowe, in which is a port, a resort of ships

Bath and Bristol

coming from Ireland, Norway, and other countries beyond sea; lest a region so fortunate in native riches should be destitute of the commerce of foreign wealth."

As to her commercial supremacy and adventuring, Mrs. J. R. Green in her *Town Life in the Fifteenth Century* has truly remarked—

"There were none who surpassed the merchants of Bristol—men who had made their town the chief depot for the wine trade of Southern France, a staple for leather, tin, and the great mart for fish of the Channel and for the salt trade of Brittany; whose cloth and leather were carried to Denmark to be exchanged for stock-fish, and to France and Spain for wine; who as early as 1420 made their way by compass to Iceland, and whose vessels were the first to enter the Levant."

A remarkable illustration of Bristol's status as a port as far back as the fourteenth century is shown in the fact that when Edward the Third, in the year 1346, called upon the great ports of England to supply him with men and ships for his wars with the French, Bristol supplied him with no less than 608 men and 22 ships, whilst London's contribution was but 662 men and 24 ships; yet Liverpool could only supply him with 1 barque and 6 men! Even as late as 1634 the difference in status between Bristol and Liverpool is strikingly shown by the fact that, whilst Charles I levied on the former "ship money" to the extent of 2000 guineas, Liverpool's portion was a beggarly £15.

Her splendid series of Charters date from the twelfth century, and she was less than thirty years after London

Bristol

in having a chief magistrate. So great was her importance in the Middle Ages that Edward III made her a county in 1373. The illustrious Edmund Burke, who represented her in Parliament from 1774 to 1780, legislated from the Bristol hustings, for his speeches delivered here have become classic. The late Lord Acton said that they were "an epoch in constitutional history. Burke then laid down for ever the law of the relations between members and their constituencies." And Lord Rosebery has affirmed that the representation of Bristol was the greatest honour received by Burke during his lifetime.

From her quay sailed the pioneer steamship, the *Great Western*, that bridged the Atlantic by steam, built to the design of the famous Brunel—an event which revolutionized ocean-going traffic.

To-day, whilst justifiably proud of her great past, she is thoroughly alive both to her present and future position as one of the great ports of the Empire. Thus she has invested in her docks, inclusive of the Royal Edward Dock at Avonmouth, a sum of over £6,000,000.

It is safe to assert, too, that there is hardly an industry that can be named but what is represented in Bristol; even though throughout the world tobacco and cocoa have alone made her name famous. Last year the former yielded its shareholders the enormous profit of over £3,000,000.

In regard to her educational equipment, she has a splendid university, due to the magnificent generosity of the Wills family, who have contributed nearly £300,000, apart from other gifts to the city.

Bath and Bristol

Bristol, it is interesting to note, was the first university to open its doors to women.

At Clifton, Bristol's glorious suburb, she possesses one of the finest public schools in England, from whence have come men whose fame has added lustre to their Alma Mater.

Such has been the growth and development of this ancient capital of the West, that well within the last century she has extended her boundaries no fewer than four times. In brief, Bristol of to-day is determined to make her future worthy of her glorious past.

CLIFTON COLLEGE

CHAPTER III

EMPIRE BUILDING

PRE-EMINENT among Bristol's many claims on the recognition of the world is that she has been a great pioneer of Empire.

Nearly twenty years prior to the advent of the Cabots on our shores, an adventuring merchant of Bristol, John Jay, who had filled the office of sheriff, and who lies buried in St. Mary Redcliffe, sent out in the year 1480 two ships of eighty tons burden, in search of the New Brazils and far Cathay.

To this early spirit of adventuring by Bristol men we have the disinterested testimony of Pedro de Ayala, of the Spanish Embassy, who, writing to the Spanish authorities in 1498, said: "The people of Bristol have for the last seven years every year sent out two, three, and four lightships in search of the Island of Brazil and the seven cities."

There is little doubt that the fame of Bristol as a great maritime centre had been carried throughout the known world by the sailors who frequented her port on their voyages to and fro across the seas. It is therefore not surprising that the great navigator, John Cabot and his family, should have sailed hither to offer their services in the quest of the unknown lands. With

Bath and Bristol

their adventurous eyes ever westward we can well imagine that he was warmly welcomed by the merchants of Bristol. Encouraged, therefore, by their support, he applied for and obtained on 5th March 1496 a patent from Henry VII empowering him and his three sons, Lewis, Sebastian, and Sanctus, to set sail, discover, and possess the new isles beyond the seas. So one May morning in that never-to-be-forgotten year of 1497, without beat of drums or flourish of trumpets, this little band of adventurous mariners embarked from Bristol in the little cockle-shell, the *Matthew*, probably less than a hundred tons burden, equipped by Bristol merchants and manned by eighteen sailors, nearly all of whom were Bristolians. Thus humbly began that epoch-making maritime achievement which "called in a New World to redress the balance of the Old," fraught with such momentous possibilities for the English race. Battling with the storms of the Atlantic, the intrepid leader John Cabot and his little crew of undaunted sailors made their historic landing in the early summer on the coast of Newfoundland. The actual spot, though conjectured, is still an unsolved geographical riddle. This at once and for ever disposes of the claim that Columbus discovered the New World, for he did not land on the southern continent till at least a year later. Thus the part played by Cabot and his brave companions has rightly become one of our national glories. All competent authorities are now in agreement that this voyage of John Cabot marks one of the greatest epochs of English history, and that he, the father of Sebastian, was the real founder of English maritime supremacy. To

Empire Building

fittingly mark so glorious a deed connected with her annals, Bristol's citizens built the noble Cabot Tower on Brandon's green and lofty hill on the four hundredth anniversary of that maritime achievement; from whose summit the silver bar of Severn can easily be seen on a clear day, and the magnificent view obtained of the city and its lovely surroundings is a sight to linger long in the memory. It was built at a cost of £3300, and the ceremonies of laying the foundation stone and the opening were performed by the late Marquess of Dufferin.

In regard to the Cabot voyage of 1497, Lorenzo Pasqualigo, writing on 11th October of that year to his brother, says—

"The Venetian, our countryman, who went with a ship from Bristol in quest of new islands, is returned, and says that seven hundred leagues hence he discovered land, the territory of the Great Cham. He coasted for three hundred leagues and landed, saw no human being, but he has brought hither to the King certain snares which had been set to catch game, and a needle for making nets; he also found some felled trees, whereupon he supposed there were inhabitants, and returned to his ship in alarm. He was three months on the voyage, and on his return he saw two islands to the starboard, but would not land, time being precious, as he was short of provisions. He that says the tides are slack and do not flow as they do here. The King of England is much pleased with this intelligence. The King has promised that in the spring our countryman shall have ten ships, armed to his order, and at his request has conceded him all the prisoners, except such as are confined for high treason, to man the

Bath and Bristol

fleet. The King has given him money wherewith to amuse himself till then, and he is now at Bristol with his wife, who is also a Venetian, and with his son. His name is Zucan Cabot, and he is styled the 'Great Admiral.' Vast honour is paid him; he dresses in silk, and these English run after him like mad people, so that he can enlist as many of them as he pleases, and a number of our own rogues besides."

Sebastian, the famous son of John Cabot, was born some say in Venice and others in Bristol. There is considerable confliction of evidence on the point, because he seems to have lied unblushingly when it suited his purpose. For example, he has stated first that he was born at Venice, and again later, when an old man, he distinctly told his friend Richard Eden that " he was borne in Brystowe, and that at iiii years ould he was carried with his father to Venice, and so returned agayne into England with his father after certayne years, whereby he was thought to have been born at Venice."

Thus through the mendacity of Sebastian the honour rightly belonging to his father, John Cabot, has for centuries been withheld. Therefore in justice all the eulogies henceforth applied to Sebastian by successive writers on maritime history must be transferred to the real discoverer, his father, John Cabot. Undoubtedly modern research into the history of the Cabots, especially the great work of Harrisse, has been destructive of the fame hitherto awarded him, and to-day he is dethroned in favour of his father as the " greatest navigator and cosmographer that ever lived."

Fired by the example of the Cabots, we find

THE "SULTANA", A TIMBER SHIP

Empire Building

Robert Thorne, an eminent Bristol merchant, urging on Henry VIII the desirability of making an attempt to find the north-west passage of the Moluccas. Said he: "With a small number of ships there might be discovered divers new lands and kingdoms, in which without doubt your Grace shall win perpetual glory and your subjects infinite profit. To which places there is left one way to discover, which is into the north."

This representation to the King was promptly acted upon, but, unfortunately, with barren results; for on 20th May 1527 he sent, Hakluyt tells us, "two fair ships well manned and victualled, having in them divers cunning men, to seek strange regions." These ships, the *Mary of Guildford* and the *Samson*, set sail from Bristol on 10th June of that year, and proceeded due north as Thorne had directed; but on 1st July a violent storm arose, which wrecked the *Samson*, with the loss of all her crew. The sister ship sailed on a little farther, but not speedily finding the wealth of Cathay, the captain lost heart on finding many great islands of ice, and returned.

Thus ended the first and only voyage of discovery in the reign of Henry VIII.

A few years later, in 1552, the trading enterprise of Bristol merchants fitted out three ships, freighted with cargoes of linen and woollen cloth, amber and jet, bound for Morocco. There they met with a hostile reception from the Portugese and Spaniards, but despite this they returned home safely. This was the pioneer voyage of Bristol to the dark continent, though in later times she had a large and thriving trade with the west coast of Africa.

Bath and Bristol

With her passion for adventuring to new lands still unquenched, we find that in the beginning of the following century "a voyage set out from the city of Bristol, at the charge of the chiefest inhabitants, with a small ship and barque for the discovery of the north part of Virginia, under the command of Martin Pring."

This daring Bristol mariner, then only twenty-three years of age, states that the voyage was undertaken through the "reasonable inducement of Richard Hakluyt, prebendary of the Cathedral, the chief furtherers of the undertaking being those public-spirited merchants of the city, Aldermen Aldworth and Whitson, and altogether a sum of £1000 was adventured on the enterprise." These vessels, judged by the standard of present-day ships, were preposterously small, and ill-fitted to face the storms that sweep the Atlantic; for the *Speedwell* was but fifty tons and the *Discoverer* only twenty.

Pring, however, fearlessly set sail on 20th March 1603, and reached the coast of North Virginia—the New England that was to be—early in June. He remained there nearly two months, lying for some time in the harbour, to which he gave the name Whitson, but which was afterwards to become memorable as "Plymouth," at which the Pilgrim Fathers landed seventeen years later.

Pring says: "We carried with us from Bristoll two excellent mastiffs, of whom the Indians were more afraid than of twenty of our men. One of the mastiffs would carry a half pike in his mouth. And one Master Thomas Bridges, a gentleman of our company, accompanied only with one of these dogs, passed six miles alone in the country, having lost his fellows, and returned safely.

Empire Building

And when we would be rid of the savages' company we would let loose the mastiffs, and suddenly without cries they would flee away."

Having closely surveyed the coast, discovered several rivers and harbours, and loaded his ships with sassafras, then a valuable medicinal plant, he set sail for England, reaching Bristol on 2nd October, when he quaintly reported the land to be "full of God's good blessings, so is the sea replenished with great abundance of excellent fish, or cod, sufficient to laden many ships."

Closely associated, too, with Bristol was Sir Ferdinando Gorges, "the Father of English Colonization in North America," who came of an honourable family long connected with Wraxall, near the city, and was moved, through information supplied him by one of the early explorers, to form a company for the colonization of America. Through his efforts a Virginia Company was established in 1606, and it was granted a charter by Charles I. "This document," says Bancroft, the American historian, "was the first colonial charter under which the English were planted in America." By the influence of Sir Ferdinando Gorges and Lord Chief Justice Popham, who had at an earlier period represented Bristol in Parliament, a subscription was opened at the Council House, Bristol, for "the plantation and inhabiting of Virginia," the contributions to extend over five years. Among those who responded to the invitation were the mayor, John Guy, and Robert Aldworth. A vessel was forthwith equipped and sent out from Bristol, sailing in September or October 1606, Hannam being appointed commander and Martin Pring master. Little is recorded, however, of its adven-

Bath and Bristol

tures save a brief note by Gorges, containing the important statement that Pring had returned with "the most exact discovery of that coast that ever came into my hands."

In 1903 a tercentenary commemoration of Pring's voyage to New England in 1603 was held by the Maine Historical Society at Portland, U.S.A. Pring became later General of the East India fleet in the year 1617. As a recognition of his services the Virginia Company in 1622 made him a freeman of the Company, and gave him shares of land there. This pioneer of Empire expansion died in 1626, and was buried in St. Stephen's Church, Bristol, where a highly elaborate monument bearing a curious old-world epitaph to his merits will be found containing the following lines :—

> "Faith was his sailes,
> His Anchor Hope. A Hope that never failes.
> His freight was Charitie, and his returne
> A fruitful practise : in this fatall urne
> His Shipp's fayre Bulck is lodged : but yet rich ladinge
> Is housed in Heaven. A Haven never fadinge."

Reverting to Virginia, we find that a grant was made on 29th February 1631 to Robert Aldworth and Giles Elbridge of twelve thousand acres of land, also a hundred acres for each person transported thither by them. Prior to which they had already purchased an island there in 1626. Subsequently that year Elbridge's son Thomas settled there ; and in December a grant of twelve thousand acres was made to Sir Ferdinando's grandson ; whilst his cousin, Thomas Gorges, became Deputy-Governor of Maine in 1640. He was greatly esteemed by the early settlers there for his good government.

Empire Building

Indeed it is said of him that "his was by far the one conspicuous, attractive personality in the province in all its early history."

Among those who sailed from Bristol for the New England was the Rev. Richard Mather and his family, who shipped in 1635 in the *James*, a little vessel of but 220 tons burden. That Bristol was taking an active and important part in the colonizing of New England is confirmed by the licence issued from Whitehall bearing date 21st July 1639, which recites that "upon the humble petition of Giles Elbridge, of the city of Bristol, merchant, praying license for exportation of about eighty passengers and some provisions formerly accustomed for the increase and support of his fishing plantation in New England, their Lordships did this day give leave unto the said Elbridge to export for New England the said eighty passengers, together with such provisions as hath been formerly accustomed, provided that he do give bond for His Majesty's use, that none of the said persons shall be shipped until publicly before the Mayor of Bristol, they have taken the oaths of allegiance and supremacy."

Meanwhile, Sir Ferdinando Gorges, with unabated vigour and enthusiasm, not content with having obtained from King James I in 1620 for his Company the extraordinary grant of the whole of North America from the Atlantic to the Pacific, but nineteen years later, in 1639, had secured from King Charles I a charter conceding to him and his heirs the entire province of Maine, New England, minus certain reservations to the Crown. Not only so, but in Bristol at the Great House, St. Augustine's, at the age of seventy-three, he drew up the charter

Bath and Bristol

of the city of Georgeana, which embodied "such and so many privileges, liberties, and freedoms as the city of Bristol"; his residence there being due to the fact that he had married the widow of Sir Hugh Smyth of Ashton Court, whose property it was. This was doubtless the last official act of this extraordinary pioneer of English colonization.

Not content with colonizing New England, the merchants of Bristol sought permission in the year 1609 from the Privy Council to found a plantation in Newfoundland, the petitioners being jointly merchants of London and Bristol. Among the local men were Humphrey Hooke, Thomas Aldworth, and Philip and John Guy. The last named, who was an eminent merchant and held in great esteem by the citizens, having represented her in Parliament and having been mayor, was appointed the first Governor of the Company. Early in May of the following year (1610), Philip and John Guy, William Colston (father of the great philanthropist), with a number of emigrants of both sexes, to say nothing of cattle, poultry, etc., were embarked in three ships that had been equipped for the purpose *en route* for the new colony. They arrived in Newfoundland in twenty-three days, and erected dwellings, storehouses, wharves, and a fort, whilst Guy built himself a mansion called Sea Forest House. Returning to Bristol in 1611, he, in the following year, took out another party of emigrants. By his will in February 1626, he left his share of the settlement to his sons, then under age.

Unfortunately, this experiment in colonization was not successful, for there appears no record of the colony's

Empire Building

existence after the year 1628. In spite of this, however, Newfoundland proved an excellent outlet for Bristol's trade, for in December 1667 the merchants and shipowners of the city petitioned the Privy Council, praying for the better protection of Newfoundland against the French and Dutch cruisers, who threatened to destroy their trade, in the course of which they asserted that the Customs duties paid at Bristol on wine, oil, and fruit brought in from Spain, Portugal, and Italy, in exchange for the fish carried to those countries, amounted to £40,000.

In addition to these links with the North American continent, Bristolians are proud that William Penn, the founder of Pennsylvania, was the son of Admiral Sir William Penn, a native of their city, who lies buried in St. Mary Redcliffe Church. In the closing years of the seventeenth century Penn was residing in Bristol, and was married to Hannah Callowhill, a Bristolian, at the Friends' Meeting House, in the Friary. It was during his stay here that it is thought probable he planned the building of the streets adjoining the Meeting House, namely, Philadelphia, Penn, Hollister, and Callowhill Streets. The mother of Penn's wife was the daughter of Dennis Hollister, on whose ground those streets were built. The Bristol Society of Friends still have in their possession the actual lease for a year of the entire province of Pennsylvania, granted by William Penn and his son preparatory to the mortgage, on which several Friends of Bristol and other places advanced them in 1708 the sum of £6600. It was also during Penn's residence in Bristol that he secured James Logan as his secretary, who accompanied him to Philadelphia and ultimately became

Bath and Bristol

its Chief Justice and Governor. Positive proof that Penn was in Bristol in 1698 is afforded by the fact that his work, *Defence of a Paper Entituled Gospel Truths,* etc., is dated, " Bristol, the 23rd of the 7th month, 1698." A copy of this rare work is in the Bristol Reference Library.

An extremely interesting relic of Penn will be found in the Civic Art Gallery—no less than a box made from the actual tree under the shade of which Penn signed the treaty with the Indians.

That Bristol has left an imperishable influence on the great northern continent of America is abundantly evident from the fact that it is commemorated by a Bristol in the Pemaquid peninsula ; and a county in Massachusetts, and towns in Rhode Island, Pennsylvania, and other states also bear its name ; and further, that her early voyages are enshrined in the classic geographical works of Hakluyt and Purchas.

CHAPTER IV

PRIVATEERING

THE city that built the saucy *Arethusa*, renowned in song, has had a famous share in the history of privateering, and for dash and gallantry in the face of overwhelming odds the sea-dogs of Bristol were bad to beat in the eventful and stirring seventeenth and eighteenth centuries.

As some misconception exists as to what were privateers, it may be as well to state that those vessels were to all intents and purposes private men-of-war, equipped not by the Government, but by private owners carrying a *letter of marque,* or licence, which empowered them to prey upon the enemy's ships. Unlike the pirate or corsair, with whom they have often been erroneously classed, they had a well-defined legal status. That they rendered magnificent service, the annals of naval warfare amply confirm. When England was at war with France and Spain in the early years of the seventeenth century, an extraordinary stimulus was given to Bristol privateering, for in the years 1626, 1627, and 1628 no fewer than sixty privateers were fitted out to harass, capture, or destroy French and Spanish merchantmen. The number of men and guns in them were out of all proportion to their size, ranging as they did from 30 to nearly 600 tons. Yet, small cockle-shells as they were, they

Bath and Bristol

successfully matched themselves against the huge galleons of Spain. Their intrepid daring is immortalized in the ballad entitled, "The Honour of Bristol," which is not unworthy to rank with the best of our maritime ballads, being in parts as heart-stirring as "Chevy Chase." It tells how about the year 1626 the *Angel Gabriel*, commanded by the famous Netheway, with forty fighting men, put to flight three Spanish ships of war, with the alleged loss to the enemy of five hundred men. The following stanzas are typical of the whole :—

> "The lusty ship of Bristol
>   Sailed out adventurously
> Against the foes of England,
>   Their strength with them to try:
> Well victualled, rigged, and manned,
>   And good provision still,
> Which made them cry to sea
>   With the *Angel Gabriel*!"

The terrible nature of the fight when they encountered the foe is indicated as follows :—

> "With that their three ships boarded us
>   Again with might and main,
> But still our noble Englishmen
>   Cried out—'A fig for Spain!'
> Though seven times they boarded us,
>   At last we showed our skill,
> And made them feel the force
>   Of our *Angel Gabriel*!"

In brief, the ballad narrates that against fearful odds the men of the *Angel Gabriel* proved more than a match for the Spaniards.

Privateering

million of those documents, which the Spanish colonists were in the habit of purchasing at dear rates from the Catholic clergy. With cynical disregard of their sacred purpose, Rogers observed that he found them useful for burning pitch off the ships' bottoms when they were careened.

Finally, after having circumnavigated the world, they reached the Thames on 14th October 1711, bringing an enormous booty, estimated at nearly £200,000. Alexander Selkirk received as his share of the plunder of this memorable expedition £800.

In the year 1739 the public prints contained the announcement that "some eminent merchants of Bristol had subscribed £5000 for the glorious purpose of fitting out privateers to go upon an expedition in quest of Spanish villains who insulted and robbed British subjects, and especially those belonging to the port of Bristol. It is expected that £5000 more will be raised at the next meeting." A year or two later, on the declaration of war with France, a tremendous stimulus was given to Bristol privateering, and a fleet of privateers was fitted out by the merchants, the largest of which was the *Bristol*, of 550 tons. These vessels met with great success and reaped fortunes for their lucky owners, and the harbour on the return of the successful vessels was a scene of great excitement and enthusiasm. One of these alone, the *Southwell*, in the first four months of her career captured no fewer than eight prizes, and the *Constantine*, another of the fleet, made three prizes in as many weeks, whilst others of the fleet were equally successful. As a consequence of the distribution of the

Bath and Bristol

large sums of prize money among the victorious crews, riotous scenes in the streets were of daily occurrence. "Nothing is seen here," said one of the Bristol journals of the time, "but rejoicing for the great number of French prizes brought in. Our sailors are in the highest of spirits, full of money, and spend their whole time in carousing, dressed out with laced hats, tassels, swords, with sword knots, and, in short, all things that can give them an opportunity of spending their money."

The daring of these Bristol sea-dogs would be well-nigh incredible were it not supported by incontrovertable facts. For example, on one occasion the *Tryall* privateer retook the *Prime Minister* of London from under the guns of five French men-of-war. This little vessel had only sixteen guns and a crew of 120 men. She subsequently brought into Bristol a Spanish prize containing gold and silver, besides a quantity of arms and ammunition.

Two of the most famous romances of English literature have immortalized the stirring period of Bristol's history in their novels—*Treasure Island* and *The Pirate*. In the latter, Mordaunt says to the captain of the *Good Hope*, "You had come north about then from the West Indies?" "Ay, ay; the vessel was the *Good Hope* of Bristol, a *letter of marque*. She had fine luck down on the Spanish Main, both with commerce and privateering, but the luck's ended with her now. My name is Clement Cleveland, captain and part owner, as I said before. I am a Bristol man born—my father was well known on the Tollsell—old Clem Cleveland of the College Green." Relating one of his

Privateering

exploits, he said, "What say you to shooting the man at the wheel, just as we run aboard of the Spaniard? So the Don was taken aback and we laid him athwart the hawse, and carried her cutlass in hand; and worth the while she was—stout brigantine—*El Santo Francisco*, bound for Porto Bello, with gold and negroes. That little bit of lead was worth twenty thousand pistoles."

A vivid idea of the dash and gallantry of these Bristol sea-dogs is conveyed by the following: In the year 1746, whilst at sea in the *Alexander*, her commander, Captain Phillips, learned that H.M.S. *Solebay*, of 38 guns, captured by a French man-of-war, was being fitted out in St. Martin's Bay, near Bordeaux, to convoy a fleet of merchantmen to the West Indies. On the strength of this information he determined to retake her, and accordingly despatched his boats to the spot with fifty of his best men, who dashed on board during the night, and after a desperate struggle with the French crew, succeeded in cutting her cables and carrying her off. Captain Phillips brought her ultimately to Bristol with 200 prisoners aboard. For this remarkable exploit he received 500 guineas, and a medal of £100 value from the King.

In daring emulation, Captain Richards of the *Bellona*, of 16 guns, two years later actually ran into the same bay, and cut from their moorings fourteen French vessels, two of which, laden with wine, were brought safely to Ireland.

This audacious feat, says the *London Chronicle*, was done in broad daylight, and within gunshot of seven French men-of-war and four frigates.

Bath and Bristol

Equally daring was the exploit narrated in the following extract from a letter written by the second captain of the *Phœnix* privateer of Bristol, dated 6th April 1758 : " It is with the greatest satisfaction I acquaint you of our success. The 3rd inst. we chased, and about ten o'clock came up with, the *Bellona* privateer of St. Malo's, mounting 18 six-pounders and 12 swivels, with 120 men. I told Captain Read if it was agreeable to him, I would board the Frenchman with the boat, which I did with five men and myself; but making use of the name of the *Tartar* man-of-war, and presenting my pistol to the captain's breast, struck them with such a panic they could not stand. My men backed me bravely, and drove them with our cutlasses like a flock of frightened sheep, when all on board the *Phœnix* thought that we were cut to pieces; but to their great surprise we soon sent them a boat-load of prisoners."

Later, a very gallant fight took place between the *Constantine* and a French privateer, the *Victoire*. Taken somewhat unawares, as he had believed the French vessel to be an English man-of-war, Captain Forsyth of the Bristol ship and his men, we are told, " behaved like English lions, and twice cleared the bowsprit, forecastle, and head, though six to one against us—even though the Frenchmen rushed the quarter-deck, and came in at the cabin windows." So severe was the fight that the French captain was killed and a great number of his men—the blood running out of the scuppers; but at length the foe sheered off, leaving, however, a blood-dyed track behind him. " Blessed be the Almighty," said Captain Forsyth,

Privateering

"I had but two wounded, who came to their quarters as soon as they were dressed by the surgeon." Thus was a victory won against great odds, for the Bristol ship had only 18 four-pounders and 46 men, whilst the Frenchman had 20 six-pounders and 250 men.

That this form of maritime adventuring, though brimful of danger, possessed an irresistible fascination, is proved by the fact that many of the vessels engaged in it were commanded by their owners, more especially when it might chance that fortune should throw in their way a treasure ship or ships, such as happily befell the *Prince Frederick* and *Duke*, privateers of Bristol. Cruising in the South Seas, these vessels intercepted and captured two Spanish treasure-ships—veritable floating gold-mines, named the *Marquis D'Antin* and *Louis Erasme*. Alluding to which the Bristol *Oracle Country Advertiser* for 28th September 1745 says—

"This week the treasure taken by the *Prince Frederick* and *Duke* privateers was transported from the Custom House in forty-five wagons through this city towards London, escorted by detachments of foot-soldiers, under the command of two lieutenants, preceded by trumpets and guarded by the ship's crews, properly armed and accoutred. They were in two divisions at a day's distance; the first, consisting of twenty-two wagons, passed from the Custom House to the Old Market (Street) on Monday, about 6 o'clock in the evening, and from thence set out the next day for London, and the remaining twenty-three did the same on Wednesday.

"Such an unusual sight drew vast numbers of spectators, so that the streets were lined with people of all

Bath and Bristol

ranks and conditions from one end of the city to the other."

The estimated value of this enormous treasure was nearly a million sterling, in addition to which there were five chests of wrought plate, a gold church in miniature, and 600 tons of cocoa.

Though privateering in Bristol continued intermittently down to the end of the eighteenth century, as shown by the evidence of an interesting epitaph in Shirehampton Churchyard, commemorating the exploits of Captain John Shaw (who was at one time commander of the *Cæsar*), yet with the close of the Seven Years War that fascinating and adventurous period of Bristol's history practically ended, abounding as it did with heroic and thrilling episodes, which it is safe to assert will never more be re-enacted.

CHAPTER V

CLIFTON: ITS BEAUTY AND ASSOCIATIONS

BRISTOL is fortunate indeed in possessing Clifton, one of the most enchantingly lovely spots in England; so richly dowered is it with natural charms that you might search the world over for its counterpart within so limited an area. Its Avon Gorge, cut through the mountain limestone, rises sheer up from the river to a height of over 300 feet as you view it from the Observatory Hill. Wondrous indeed is the sight in May or June of these remarkable rocks, clothed on the Somerset side of the river with the exquisite hanging woods of Leigh; spanned by that triumph of Brunel's engineering skill, the Suspension Bridge, whose graceful fabric appears to hang between heaven and earth, so gossamer-like it looks. Yet it weighs nearly 1500 tons, and its length from pier to pier is 702 feet, whilst its height from high-water mark of the Avon below is 245 feet. From the vantage-point of Observatory Hill one of the noblest and most extensive views is obtainable, for without the aid of a field-glass the spectator can see from the Mendips to the Blorenge and Sugar-loaf at Abergavenny, a distance of 40 miles at least. Clark Russell, the well-known novelist of the sea, eloquently describes in his *Jack's Courtship* the loveliness of this beauty spot of England. Says the hero:

Bath and Bristol

"You may talk as you please about the beauty of foreign parts. I have seen some grand shows in that way in my time, as what sailor has not? But had I never viewed anything finer than Clifton — that part, I mean, which they call the Gorge—I should still be able to boast of having beheld as lovely a bit of nature as any part of the world has to offer. What fixes it in my memory was the sunset. I had tumbled into an open fly—quite a genteel turn-out—along with my portmanteau, and when we had climbed a steep hill and got on top of it, and rolled along some distance, I stood up and saw a sky full of the magnificence of a score of glorious colours, against which the heaviest foliage and green heights which tower above the valley, in whose heart the silver Avon (at flood-tide, mind you) winds like a stream of mercury, stood out dark, massive, dense, the gold of the sky trembling among the fibrine of the wooded acclivities; and layers or folds of emerald, sapphire, rose, scarlet, like incandescent iron, sun-bright effulgence, like that of molten steel in a retort swept by a hurricane of a steam-created blast, stretching their most beautiful lengths along until their extremities faded in the black vapour of a huge cloud, from whose sooty belly green sparks of lightning were crackling and glittering, whilst the thunder moaned like the voice of a lion heard roaring in pain in some distant resonant forest."

On this same hill are the remains of one of those prehistoric camps or fortresses thrown up by the Belgæ, declared by Cæsar to have been the most powerful and the least civilized of all the Gallic tribes. Immediately opposite on the other side of the Avon is another of

Clifton

these camps known as Stokesleigh|; whilst immediately to its left is the extremely lovely Nightingale Valley eulogized by Ruskin, who spent some weeks here with his parents about 1840, for, writing to a friend, he says : " I don't wonder at your admiring Clifton. It is certainly the finest piece of limestone scenery in the kingdom. Did you ever find out the dingle running up through the cliffs on the south [sic] side of the river, opposite St. Vincent's? When the leaves are on, there are pieces of Ruysdael study of rock there, with the noble cliff through the breaks of foliage, quite intoxicating."

The delightful woods of Leigh have been the haunt and nursery of many famous artists, including Müller, Danby, Pyne, and the Fripps. Among those who have explored its beauties was De Quincey, who mentions in one of his *Letters*, whilst residing in Bristol, that Hartley Coleridge had dined with him. " And I gained his special favour, I believe, by taking him—at the risk of our respective necks—through every dell and tangled path of Leigh Wood."

A few years ago, through the initiative of Mr. James Baker, and the President of the Bristol and Gloucestershire Archæological Society, committees were formed to rescue from destruction this primeval woodland and its prehistoric camp ;—ample evidence of the latter's neolithic occupation has been discovered. This was happily successful through the splendid generosity of Mr. G. A. Wills, and both are now under the guardianship of the National Trust. The magnificent beauty of the Avon Gorge and the hanging woods of Leigh do not exhaust the beauty assets of Clifton, for it possesses, too, its

Bath and Bristol

glorious Downs—probably the noblest pleasure-ground in Europe adjacent to a great centre of commerce, comprising as it does no less than 442 acres—

> "Where salt winds from the channel blow,
> And make your English pulses glow."

Well might a writer in *St. James's Gazette* say: "People travel far and wide and cross the sea to explore the world, to admire the romantic acclivities of Ponte Asino, or Spitz Mondschein, or any other equally celebrated spot. They leave to humbler crowds a scene within two hours of London as lovely as a dream: a world of deep ravines, of fair downs, and wooded slopes, undulating to the blue hills of Wales and to that distant bar of light which is the sea. . . . And yet this could only be England—this wide and nobly wooded space; while in the ravine below the wonderful Clifton bridge hangs, slung midway between heaven and earth, between light and shadow, reaching from height to height."

Perhaps, however, the most graphic picture yet written of Clifton's Downs is contained in William Black's novel, *The Strange Adventures of a House Boat*, as follows: "After luncheon we got a carriage and drove away out to the famous Downs, of which Bristol is very naturally proud. It was a beautiful afternoon—a light westerly wind tempering the hot glare of the sun; and there was everywhere a summer-like profusion of foliage and blossom—of red and white hawthorn, of purple lilac and golden laburnum—in the pretty gardens that front the long ascending Whiteladies Road. Arrived at the Downs, we of course proceeded on foot, across the undulating pasture-land

Clifton

bestarred with squat hawthorn-bushes that were now all powdered over with pink-white or cream-white bloom. The view from these heights was magnificent: beyond the luxuriant woods in the neighbourhood of the Avon, which were all golden-green in the warm afternoon light, the wide landscape retreated fold upon fold and ridge upon ridge to the high horizon line, becoming bluer and bluer till lost in the pale southern sky. It was only here or there some far hill or hamlet, some church spire or wood-crowned knoll, caught that golden glow, and shone faint and dim; mere distance subdued all local colour; and the successive landscape waves that rolled out to the horizon were but so many different shades of atmospheric azure, lightening or deepening according to the nature of the country. Of topographical knowledge we had none; we only knew that this was a bit of England; and a very fair and pleasant sight it seemed to be."

It is noteworthy too, showing Clifton's antiquity, that its commanding position strategetically attracted the attention of the Romans, for they appear to have stationed here a detachment of the second legion, which brought into being a village, inhabited partly by the legionaries themselves, and partly by Britons under their protection. Evidences of such a Roman occupation were found in the close of the eighteenth century in the shape of coins, among others those of Constantine, Nero, Domitian, and Trajan; also relics of Roman pottery, including a curious urn with two handles. Thus though the Clifton Camp was originally constructed by the Belgæ, that the Romans subsequently occupied it is archæologically evident from the traces of their presence found there. Reverting to

Bath and Bristol

the literary associations connected with the Downs, we find the famous poet, Alexander Pope, when taking the Hotwell waters in 1739, writing to his friend Martha Blount as follows :—

"Upon the top of those high rocks by the Hotwells, which I have described to you, there runs on one side a large down of fine turf for about three miles. It looks too frightful to approach the brink and look down upon the river ; but in many parts of this down the valleys descend gently, and you see all along the windings of the stream, and the opening of the rocks, which turn and close in upon you, from space to space, for several miles towards the sea. There is first, near Bristol, a little village upon this down, called Clifton, where are very pretty lodging-houses, overlooking all the woody hills, and steep cliffs, very green valleys, within half a mile of the Wells, where in summer it is most delicious walking and riding, for the plain extends one way many miles."

Few of the present generation of Bristolians are aware that in Smollett's *Humphry Clinker* the heroine of that famous novel, Miss Lydia Melford, gives us a charming picture of the Downs in her day : "We set out for Bath to-morrow, and I am almost sorry for it, as I begin to be in love with solitude ; and this is a charming romantic place. The air is so pure, the Downs so agreeable, the furze in full blossom, the ground enamelled with daisies, primroses, and cowslips ; all the trees bursting into leaves, and the hedges already clothed with their vernal livery. . . . The groves resound with the notes of the blackbird, thrush, and linnet ; and all night long sweet Philomel pours forth her

IN LEIGH WOODS

Clifton

ravishing delightful song. Then, for variety, we go down to the *nymph of Bristol Spring*, where the company is assembled before dinner, so good-natured, so free and easy; there we drink the water, so clear, so mild, so charmingly mawkish. There the sun is so cheerful and warm, the weather so soft, the walk so agreeable, the prospect so amusing; and the ships and boats going up and down the river close under the windows of the Pump Room, afford such an enchanting variety of moving pictures as requires a much abler pen than mine to describe."

Among famous literary ladies who have paid tribute to the beauty of Clifton's Downs are Maria Edgeworth, Mrs. Thrale, Lady Hesketh, and Harriet Martineau, the first of whom on arriving here in 1793, and writing to her uncle, says: "We live very near the Downs, where we have almost every day charming walks, and all the children go bounding about over hill and dale along with us."

To Clifton came, too, Mrs. Thrale, the intimate friend of Dr. Johnson, in 1820, where she resided at 36 Royal York Crescent. Writing from there she says: "Dear Mrs. Willoughby will be glad to hear I am where I shall be on the sweet Downs." There she died in the following year.

In the closing years of the eighteenth century the poet Cowper's charming cousin, the beautiful Lady Hesketh, was residing in Clifton. Writing in September 1799 to a friend, she says: "I left Bath last Thursday, and came to this most charming place, Clifton Hill, where I design to pass some time, and which is just now

Bath and Bristol

in great beauty, the woods which crown these charming rocks being as green as in June, and the verdure of the whole country intense! I think you would be greatly charmed and delighted could you see the sweet, sublime, yet peaceful views which I enjoy. Nature has been so profuse in her bounties in the disposition of the ground and the happy combination of wood, water, rocks, etc., that it is always preferable to any other place." From Clifton she indited many charming letters to Cowper, and her vivacity of disposition did much to enliven his habitual melancholy. She died in 1807, and lies buried in Bristol Cathedral.

Harriet Martineau, who spent her schooldays here, also speaks in rapturous admiration of the Downs and Leigh Woods.

Later, Charles Kingsley was here at school, and he, too, loved to roam over the Downs in quest of botanical treasures. And was it not in struggling against a high wind across these Downs in quest of the missing Arabella Allen that Sam Weller in *Pickwick Papers* wondered whether it was always necessary to hold your hat on with both hands in that part of the country, and where, too, he had his lively and amusing altercation with the surly groom—

"Mornin', old friend," said Sam.

"Arternoon, you mean," replied the groom, casting a surly look at Sam.

"You're wery right, old friend," said Sam, "I *do* mean arternoon. How are you?"

"Why, I don't find myself much the better for seeing of you," replied the ill-tempered groom.

Clifton

"That's wery odd—that is," said Sam, "for you look so uncommon cheerful, and seem altogether so lively, that it does vun's heart good to see you."

The surly groom looked surlier still at this.

Sam then inquired with a countenance of great anxiety whether his master's name was not Walker.

"No, it ain't," said the groom.

"Nor Brown, I s'pose?" said Sam.

"No, it ain't."

"Nor Vilson?"

"No, nor that neither," said the groom.

"Vell," replied Sam, "then I'm mistaken, and he hasn't got the honour o' my acquaintance, which I thought he had. Don't vait here out o' compliment to me," said Sam, as the groom wheeled in the barrow and prepared to shut the gate. "Ease afore ceremony, old boy; I'll excuse you."

"I'd knock your head off for half a crown," said the surly groom, bolting one half of the gate.

"Couldn't afford to have it done on those terms," rejoined Sam. "It 'ud be worth a life's board and vages at least, to you, and 'ud be cheap at that. Make my compliments indoors. Tell 'em not to vait dinner for me, and say they needn't mind puttin' any by, for it'll be cold afore I come in."

Muttering a fervent desire to damage somebody's head, the groom retired, slamming the door angrily after him, wholly unheeding Sam's affectionate request that he would leave him a lock of his hair.

In dealing with Clifton we must not forget its one-time famous spa at the Hotwells, which was in the

Bath and Bristol

eighteenth century a rival in popularity to its sister spa of Bath. The earliest mention of this spa is by the celebrated Bristol itinerant, William Wycestre, who in the year 1460 speaks of the waters gushing from the base of St. Vincent's Rock, they being then unenclosed, though he appears to have been ignorant of their medicinal qualities. This is traditionally said to have been accidentally discovered by some sailors about 1630, who, washing in the water at low tides and drinking freely of it, were healed of the scurvy they had contracted. That its curative fame soon spread is evident, for it is alluded to in the " Itinerary of Three Gentlemen of the Military Company of Norwich," who four years later visited the city—

"After we had taken a full and contentive view of this sweet city (Bristol) and of her compass, fenced in with strong walls and gates, we then desired to know what was near unto her remarkable.

"Within a mile and a half of her, by the Haven's channel, we found a strange hot well, which came gushing out of a mighty stony rock into the stream, so nigh thereto that every tide it overflows it. To it we descended by a rocky and steep, winding, and craggy way, near 200 slippery steps, which place, when the tide is gone, *never wants good store of company to wash in this well, and to drink of that warm and medicinal water ; and for its rarity divers carry it away with them.* When we had felt and tasted the rare excellency of these waters, we mounted up again, and for the space of an hour or two laid aside our commanding posture and turned pioneers, to dig and delve for some glittering bastard diamond stones which that hill plentifully afforded."

Clifton

These "Bristol diamonds" are often referred to by various writers. In a satire by Bishop Hall of Norwich, he says—

> "Nor can good Myson wear on his left hand
> A signet ring of *Bristol Diamond.*"

And in one of the State Papers of the reign of James I, mention is made of these stones of brilliant quartz being supplied to Lord Cecil for the decoration of the King's palace.

Evelyn of *Diary* fame, who visited Clifton in 1655, mentions in it: "What was most stupendous to me was the rock of St. Vincent, the precipice whereof is equal to anything of that nature I have seen in the most confragous cataracts of the Alps, the river gliding between them of an extraordinary depth. Here we went searching for diamonds."

Among these early visitors to the Hotwells was the celebrated statesman, Bulstrode Whitelocke; for already the Hotwells water was famed as a cure for leprosy and stone. Quaint old Fuller in his *Worthies* eulogizes the water as "sovereign for sores and sicknesses."

In July 1677 Queen Catherine came over from Bath, and having dined, she proceeded in her coach to the Hotwells, attended by the gallant Earl of Ossory, and took a draught from the spring.

Defoe speaks in his day of the vast number of bottles made in the Bristol Glasshouses that were used for sending the water of St. Vincent's Rock, not only all over England, but all over the world. In Fanny Burney's *Evelina* she pictures the Hotwells of her time.

Bath and Bristol

Amongst distinguished visitors who flocked to the Hotwells was London's famous Lord Mayor Beckford, who was cured of diabetes in thirteen weeks. Here, too, came Addison the poet, Bishop Ken, the famous hymnologist; Gilbert White of Selborne; John Wesley, the Duchess of Marlborough, the Duchess of Kent, and many others of the rank and fashion of the time.

So great was the reputation of the Hotwells that it was quite customary for distinguished visitors to give breakfasts, which were numerously attended. To provide accommodation for the visitors thus attracted, Dowry Square was built about 1746. So great, indeed, was the fashionable throng that resorted to the Hotwells, that a firm of London lace dealers, scenting business, brought down their wares, among their items being "Lappet heads, from six guineas a pair to a hundred. Ruffles for gentlemen, from two to sixteen guineas."

In 1754, riding on Durdham Down was so popular with the Hotwells visitors that it is stated—"the best lady attending the Hotwell will not refuse riding behind a man, for such is the custom of the country."

The popularity of the Hotwells water in the early years of the eighteenth century is proved by the following very curious advertisement from the *London Weekly Journal* of 30th April 1726: "Bristol Hotwell water, fresh from the Wells, will be sold and delivered to any part of the town at six shillings per dozen, with the bottles, from Mr. Richard Bristow's, goldsmith, at the Three Bells, near Bride Lane, Fleet Street. These bottles are of the largest size, and by the extraordinary

Clifton

favour of the winds arrived but the last week in *eight days* from Bristol."

The reader will note two remarkable statements in this advertisement—first, the occupation of the vendor, and, secondly, the time the water took to reach London from Bristol. Its continued popularity may be gauged from the fact that in 1767 so great was the demand that it was cried in the streets every morning like milk.

Unfortunately, in 1790, owing to the Merchants' Society having raised the rent, and the avaricious nature of the then keeper of the Hotwells spring, the charges became so exorbitant—six-and-twenty shillings per month for every person—that the upper-class families who had hitherto flocked to the Hotwells in pursuit of health or pleasure were driven away, so that by the beginning of the nineteenth century this famous spa became practically deserted. One of its latest visitors was the beautiful Mrs. Sheridan, who, falling into a rapid consumption, was brought here in the vain hope that the waters would restore her to health. Here she passed away in her husband's arms on 28th June 1792, and was interred in Wells Cathedral. There is a story told, which it is to be hoped is untrue, that whilst taking an airing on the Downs her carriage and horses were seized by her husband's creditors, this painful event materially hastening her end.

Some Famous Clifton Houses

The homes and haunts of those who have left ineffaceable imprints on the sands of time will ever have for

Bath and Bristol

mankind a profound and imperishable interest. Thus it is well, lest the fever of commerce and the haste to be rich should shut out from our ken "the vision and the faculty divine," that we should be reminded how the very locality in which we may live is interwoven with other and greater lives who have either in thought or action enriched the country of their birth by their achievements.

Equipped then with this spirit, and with the torch of sympathetic imagination, let us for a brief while make a pilgrimage to Clifton's homes of departed greatness. Starting from the top of Park Street and passing down Berkeley Place, we speedily arrive at Clifton Hill, mounting which we find on our left Bellevue, and at No. 2 we pause reverently, for within its plain, solid exterior lived as schoolboys two of the noblest defenders of Empire that England ever possessed—Lord Lawrence and Sir Henry Lawrence; the former the "Saviour of India," the latter the heroic defender of Lucknow, immortalized by Tennyson. In the early years of the nineteenth century they might have been seen daily wending their way across Brandon Hill to their school in College Green. A tablet fittingly marks the house.

Retracing our steps we ascend the hill, upon whose crown stands, four-square to the winds of heaven, a fine type of the solidity of Early Georgian architecture, faced with Bath stone, erected by Paul Fisher, a wealthy merchant of Bristol, in 1747. In this mansion lived in happy boyhood and early manhood the famous writer and art historian, John Addington Symonds, author of the monumental work, among others from his gifted

Clifton

pen, *The Renaissance of Italy*. Many famous guests have been entertained in that hospitable and cultured home of other days : Benjamin Jowett, the great Platonian scholar and Master of Balliol ; John Conington, Thomas Woolner, the distinguished sculptor ; and the world-famous Swedish nightingale, Jenny Lind, whose exquisite singing moved Symonds to the soul and filled his eyes with tears. Robert Louis Stevenson, whose friend he was, has given him immortality in *Talk and Talkers* as Opalstein.

Turning into Clifton Place, we pause again, for here at the Manor House, now an hotel, lived John Sterling, one of the celebrated Cambridge "Apostles." Here he wrote his little book of poems and his famous review of Carlyle in the *Westminster Review*, which gave such intense pleasure to the Sage of Chelsea. Carlyle subsequently paid the debt of gratitude with interest by writing Sterling's life. Whilst Sterling was living there he officiated at the marriage of his fellow "Apostle," Frederick Denison Maurice, at Clifton Church, and entertained Lord Houghton, another of that distinguished brotherhood.

Resuming our pilgrimage, we skirt the boundary of the parish churchyard, wherein lie the remains, among others, of Ann Yearsley, the Bristol milkwoman poetess, whose fame was due to the disinterested friendship of Hannah More ; and Vincent Stuckey Lean, the noble benefactor who gave Bristol its magnificent Reference Library in College Green. Passing onwards, we soon reach Cornwallis House. This was formerly the home of Thomas Wedgwood, the first photographer, son of the great potter of Etruria, the true and helpful friend of Dr. Thomas Beddoes, Sir Humphry Davy, and last, but not least, of S. T. Coleridge, on whom he settled an annuity. Proceeding up Regent Street, we turn into the magnificently built Royal York Crescent, halting at No. 36, for here lived and died Mrs. Thrale, Dr. Johnson's intimate and vivacious friend. To her, indeed, all Johnsonian students are deeply indebted for the many interesting sidelights thrown on Bozzy's idol. A few steps farther bring us to No. 25, the early home of Field-Marshal Lord Roberts, whose father, Sir Abraham, lived and died there. A tablet records the association, unveiled by his famous son. Proceeding to its extreme end we again halt, for here at No. 3 was educated the fascinating consort of Napoleon III — the Empress Eugénie, who delighted in afterlife to recall the happy days she had spent there, and the lovely view of the green hills of Somerset, crowned by Dundry's noble tower.

Facing us as we leave the Crescent is Prince's Buildings, several of which have from time to time been occupied by famous visitors. In the closing years of the eighteenth century Maria Edgeworth and her family, and early in the nineteenth the illustrious Napiers, took up their abode at No. 14. Their mother, Lady Sarah Lennox—one of the loveliest women of her time—it will be remembered, might have become Queen of England by marrying George III. Here she was visited by her kinsman Charles Fox, the statesman. Whilst residing there her husband died of consumption, and was buried in the God's Acre at Redland Green. There is a tablet

Clifton

to his memory in the porch of the chapel. At No. 4 the poet Crabbe stayed during the terrible Bristol Riots of 1831. Proceeding on our way, we turn into Caledonia Place, for at No. 16 resided for some months in 1852 the great Macaulay; a tablet recording the fact was placed there in 1903, unveiled by the late Lord Avebury. Macaulay's mother was a Bristolian, her maiden name being Selina Mills, and she was a pupil and lifelong friend of Hannah More. The latter died but a couple of hundred yards from the spot, at No. 4 Windsor Terrace, and with her, when a child, Macaulay spent many delightful visits at Barley Wood, Wrington. Passing on, we arrive at Gloucester Row. At No. 8 resided, during his Canonry of Bristol Cathedral, the witty Sydney Smith. Taking the bypath across Clifton Down opposite, we are at Canynge Road, and on its right, adjoining Harley Lodge, we find Penrose Cottage, the one-time home of Walter Savage Landor. Writing to Southey in 1838, he says : " It was my intention to return at the end of the month to Clifton. I have a great love for Clifton above all places in England." Proceeding down Clifton Park Road, and turning to the right, we halt at No. 15 Vyvyan Terrace, where lived and died the celebrated author of *The Canterbury Tales*—Harriett Lee. These tales influenced Lord Byron in his youth, and to their writer he gracefully acknowledged his indebtedness in his " Werner." William Godwin, the father-in-law of Shelley, was an unsuccessful suitor for her hand.

Once more retracing our steps, we finish our pilgrimage at No. 3 Rodney Place, a century ago the home of Dr. Thomas Beddoes, an original thinker whose work

Bath and Bristol

has never received adequate justice, the friend, too, of that brilliant literary coterie that foregathered in Bristol during the closing years of the eighteenth century. He linked himself with the Edgeworth family by marrying Maria Edgeworth's sister Anna. Their son, the eccentric Thomas Lovell Beddoes, who has left no ignoble name in the history of English poetry, was the gifted author of "The Bride's Tragedy" and "Death's Jest Book." Here lived with the Beddoes family the afterwards world-famous chemist, Sir Humphry Davy, then on the threshold of his brilliant achievements in the domain of physical science. Truly fortunate was he, too, in being the familiar friend of Coleridge, Southey, and the Wedgwoods, all of whom were a constant stimulus and inspiration to him in his work here in Bristol. A tablet commemorating the unique associations of this home of other days was unveiled in 1906 by Signor Marconi, of wireless telegraphy fame, who eulogized Davy's great contributions to physical science.

SUSPENSION BRIDGE, CLIFTON

CHAPTER VI

CHURCHES AND THEIR ASSOCIATIONS

IF a city's importance is estimated by the splendour and number of her parish churches, what city in the Empire, save London, can surpass Bristol ? Rich indeed is she in ecclesiastical wealth of architectural beauty, evidencing the piety and munificence of her merchant princes of the past. In a brief survey of some of the most notable of Bristol's churches, the mother church of the diocese must in the natural order of things claim precedence. Not, however, because the Cathedral is the most architecturally beautiful, for she is outshone by her stately daughter, St. Mary Redcliffe ; yet notwithstanding, the Cathedral church of Bristol is an extremely interesting building that deserves and repays the most careful inspection. It was originally built as an Abbey for the Augustinian Canons in 1142 by Robert Fitzharding, a progenitor of the great baronial family of Berkeley, whose history is so interwoven with that of Bristol. This Abbey Church of St. Augustine was consecrated in 1148 by four bishops. The only important remains of the original structure are the glorious Chapter House, considered one of the most perfect specimens of Anglo-Norman building in existence ; the lower portion of the magnificent great gateway, the gateway in the Lower College Green, by which

Bath and Bristol

access was obtained to the Abbot's lodgings; and the lower walls of the transepts: these nearly exhaust what remains of the original Abbey.

The Cathedral is charmingly situated fronting the grassy tree-surrounded College Green—one of those delightful open spaces of the city that arrests and soothes the jaded eyes of the sight-seer. On this very green, Tyndall, the famous translator of the New Testament and martyr, was wont to preach to the crowds who assembled there. At a much later date it was the favourite promenade of the youth of Bristol, Chatterton among others. It was he who said a genius was lost in the minutæ of the carving of the great gateway. Whilst the exterior of the Cathedral, as compared with Wells, Gloucester, or York, is not particularly impressive, yet it possesses a certain massive grandeur when viewed from the harbour on its south side by reason of its elevation above the waterway, and the low-lying ground in its vicinity. That it possesses undeniable architectural merits is evidenced from the testimony of that scholarly art historian and critic, John Addington Symonds, who on visiting it immediately after a continental tour says: " On entering the Cathedral and seeing its beautiful bare aisles, I felt the whole superiority of English architecture over Belgian and even German. The massive mullions and exquisite tracery of the windows, the grand roof with its clustered spandrels and lacy boss-work, the harmony of the parts produced by greater length, the purity of the bay arches and their moulded columns—all combine to exalt Bristol Cathedral over any I have yet seen abroad."

BRISTOL CATHEDRAL, WEST FRONT

Churches

Among features of interest in its interior, the Elder Lady Chapel, considered to be the work of Abbot David, whose rule extended from 1215–1234, should not be missed, for it contains some very curious and grotesque sculptures. The reconstruction of the Cathedral was commenced by Abbot Knowle, whose tenure of office was between 1306–1332, during which he rebuilt the eastern portion of the choir with its two aisles and Lady Chapel. The central tower was the work of John Newland or Nailheart, between 1481 and 1515. As an example of pure decorated architecture, note the intricate and beautiful design of the east window, some of the glass of which dates from the early fourteenth century. Here, too, at the east end of the south aisle is the Berkeley Chapel, its name due to the belief that it was founded in 1309 by Thomas, Lord Berkeley, as a chantry to the memory of his wife, who died in that year. A curiously interesting feature of this Cathedral is the uniform height of the vaulting of the central and the two side aisles, though different in construction, being at their highest points exactly at the same elevation from the ground, a peculiar architectural deviation not found elsewhere, though generally considered to be amply justified by reason of the happy effect produced. This highly original work of Abbot Knowle enabled him to dispense with the triforium and clerestory. Noteworthy indeed is the vaulting of those side aisles.

The Chapter House with its pillared vestibule contains some most interesting Norman work. The arches of the latter spring from clustered columns with cushioned capitals, and are studded with nail-head ornaments. This

Bath and Bristol

annexe of the Cathedral possesses a wealth of architectural enrichment. In the Lower College Green there is still to be seen the ancient gateway or entrance to the Abbot's lodgings, which is earlier in date than the beautiful main gateway above. This latter dates from the twelfth century, though the superstructure over the arch is probably late fifteenth-century work. During the present generation most important extensions have been made to this fine old building, inclusive of the nave and the western towers.

Within the Cathedral are many interesting tombs and monuments, the tombs of the Berkeley family being especially noticeable; among which is that of Robert de Berkeley, one of the barons who rebelled against King John and forced him to grant the Magna Charta. There is also an altar tomb to the memory of Thomas, Lord Berkeley, who was with Henry III at the siege of Kenilworth Castle. "He was much skilled in running at the ring, and his elder years were exercised at jousts and tournaments." Among other memorials may be mentioned that of Bishop Butler of "Analogy" fame, whose fine epitaph, considered one of the best in the language, was written by Southey. Butler, it will be remembered, was Bishop of the diocese for twelve years.

The poet Mason's wife is memorialized by the famous lines commencing—

"Take, holy earth, all that my soul holds dear."

The final lines of this famous epitaph were written by his friend Gray of "Elegy" celebrity, who was dissatisfied by Mason's lame ending, as follows :—

Churches

> "Tell them, tho' 'tis an awful thing to die
>   ('Twas ev'n to thee), yet, the dread path once trod,
> Heaven lifts its everlasting portals high
> And bids 'the pure in heart behold their God.'"

Two famous personal links with eighteenth-century men of letters are here interred—Sterne's "Eliza," Mrs. Draper, who died at Clifton and has a carved mural monument by Bacon, the sculptor; and Lady Hesketh, the beautiful and charming cousin of Cowper, the poet, whose companionship and correspondence did so much to enliven his habitual melancholy. These memorials are now in the cloisters. Here, too, is an interesting tablet to the Porter family, a member of whom was the author of the *Scottish Chiefs*, which tradition says inspired the Wizard of the North to write his immortal "Waverley" series of novels.

Fittingly commemorated in a noble epitaph by Dr. James Martineau is the life and work of that saintly social reformer, Mary Carpenter, whose career was spent in seeking to save that which was lost—the uncared-for children of the streets—

> "'Twas she first drew our city waifs and strays
>   Within the tending of the Christian fold,
> With looks of love for the averted gaze
>   Of a world prompt to scourge and shrill to scold."

Among arresting memorials to departed worthies, visitors will not fail to notice those to Richard Hakluyt, Sydney Smith, and Hugh Conway. For over thirty years, Hakluyt was a prebendary of this cathedral. To have had the "proser Homer of the English nation" and the prince of cosmographers so associated with the building adds, indeed, a personal lustre to it.

Notable also is its association with the witty canon, Sydney Smith, beloved of the laity for his brilliant and delightful conversation bubbling over with wit and good sense, who came here in 1828, and gave the Corporation such a dose of toleration that he nearly turned the turtle on their stomachs.

À propos of his appointment, he found the verger had just retired in affluent circumstances, which led him to remark to a friend that he had "never before so fully realized the truth of that passage in the Psalms, 'I had rather be a door-keeper in the house of my God than to dwell in the tents of wickedness.'"

A brilliant career untimely cut short is fittingly memoralized in the tablet to the Bristol author of *Called Back*, "Hugh Conway" (Fred Fargus).

Nor must we forget the name of Emma Marshall, the writer of *In Colston's Days*, *The Tower on the Cliff*, *Bristol Diamonds*, and dozens of other pure and wholesome stories for the young, "the high and pure quality of whose literary work" should, as Canon Ainger remarked, be "a means of awakening and cultivating a taste for history and literature throughout the English-speaking world."

Worthy of remembrance, too, associated with Bristol Cathedral is that fine Biblical scholar, Charles John Ellicott, who in 1863 was Bishop of the united Sees of Gloucester and Bristol, and during his tenure of office endeared himself to all classes of the community by his

Churches

Christian graces. His death occurred in 1905 at the great age of eighty-four, and the beautiful reredos in the cathedral, erected by his many friends, testifies to their affectionate appreciation of his labours.

Green also is the memory of that delightful and cultured man, Alfred Ainger, canon there for so many years, whose exquisite reading both then and as Master of the Temple, was a lesson in elocution of the finest kind. As a friend of George Dumaurier, the famous *Punch* artist, he inspired many of his finest drawings.

A portrait bust commemorates William Müller, the eminent Bristol artist, who, after giving magnificent promise of future artistic achievement, died on the threshold of his fame at the early age of thirty-three.

Last, but not least, among these tributes to the departed is that to John Latimer, the Historian of Bristol, who harvested such a wealth of interesting facts in his *Annals of Bristol*, which have made all interested in her history deeply his debtor.

Among notable visits paid to the cathedral we must not forget those of Royalty : Edward I worshipped here in 1284, Edward IV in 1474, Henry VII in 1486, Queen Elizabeth in 1574, Anne of Denmark in 1613, and Charles I in 1643, whose son and heir accompanied him. On one occasion Archbishop Cranmer preached here in the year 1532, and nearly two centuries later came John Wesley to hear *The Messiah* in 1758, when he doubted whether " that congregation was ever so serious at a sermon as they were during this performance."

In closing, the visitor should not omit to inspect the

misereres, twenty-eight in number, many of which are of much interest, some illustrating the *History of Reynard the Fox.*

St. Mary Redcliffe

Interesting, however, as the Mother Church of the diocese may be, she is architecturally eclipsed by the magnificent church of St. Mary Redcliffe, "the pride of Brislowe and the Western Londe," which in a city of churches, and viewed from the vantage-point of Brandon's green and lofty hill, justifies the eulogy of Queen Elizabeth, who, when visiting Bristol in 1574, pronounced it to be the "fairest, the goodliest, and most famous parish church in England." The perpendicular form of architecture is here seen in its highest perfection. In completeness of parts, grandeur of proportion, and finish of detail, the building partakes of the character of a cathedral church.

The wealth of carving in its porches, more particularly the famous north porch, the panelled walls, flying buttresses, trefoiled parapet and mural pinnacles, the storeys of windows with their elegant tracery, the magnificent tower and spire, triple-aisled transepts, long and lofty nave and chancel, tall clustered columns and graceful arches, groined roof with literally more than a thousand bosses of which no two are alike, together with the Lady Chapel and undercroft, are features that fully entitle it to rank architecturally with at least the lesser cathedrals of England. Why its magnificent proportions did not elevate it to that position instead of its neighbour,

THE CLOISTERS, BRISTOL CATHEDRAL

Churches

St. Austin's of College Green, is answered by Fuller, of *Worthies*' fame, who says, "that the church was not sufficiently accommodated like St. Augustine's with public buildings about it for the palace of a Dean or Chapter." This quaint authority further adds that, "as the town of Hague in Holland would never be built about, as accounting it more credit to be the biggest of villages in Europe than a lesser city, so Redcliffe Church esteemeth it a greater grace to lead the van of all parochial churches, than to follow in the rear after many cathedral churches in England."

One of the earliest allusions to this church of Redcliffe appears in 1232 A.D., at which time, by arrangement of Bishop Joceline (who built the west front of Wells Cathedral), a reconciliation was here effected between William de Blois, Bishop of Worcester, and the Abbot of Tewkesbury, who had been at discord. From structural evidence, authorities consider that the present church is the third which has been built on the spot. The original church is attributed to the great baronial family of Berkeley. The second, or Early English Church, is credited to the munificence of Simon de Burton, who was Mayor of Bristol no less than five times. Finally, a later and more splendid church was built by the elder and younger Canynges; the former in 1376, it is stated, "built the body of Redcliffe Church from the cross aisle downwards." In 1445, as the city records relate, during a terrible storm of thunder and lightning the spire was struck down, and falling on the body of the fabric injured it so much that extensive rebuilding was necessary. This was taken in hand by the younger William Canynge, and with what success the present superb edifice attests.

Chatterton has boded forth an imaginative picture of the opening ceremony of this newly-built church—

> "When that bright sun along the sky had sent his ruddy light,
> And fairies hid in oxlip cups till wished approach of night;
> The matin bell, with shrilly sound, re-echoed through the air;
> A troop of holy friars did for Jesus' mass prepare;
> Around the high unsainted church with holy relics went,
> And every door and post about with godly things besprent.
> Then Carpenter in scarlet dress'd and mitred holily,
> From Master Cannyng his great house with rosary did hie;
> Before him went a throng of friars who did the mass-song sing,
> Behind him Master Cannyng came trick'd like a barbed king,
> And then a row of holy friars who did the mass-song sound,
> The procurators and church reeves next pressed the holy ground . . .
> Then Carpenter did purify the church to God for aye
> With holy masses and good psalms which he therein did say . . .
> And all did go to Cannyng's house an interlude to play,
> And drunk his wine and ale so good, and pray for him for aye."

The greatest glory of the church is undoubtedly its exquisitely beautiful North Porch. The festooned and interwoven foliage of the doorway, the voluptuously decorated windows, panelled buttresses, and crocketed pedimental niches of this entrance, present in combination an intricacy of design and an elaboration of detail and finish, that challenges this England of ours to show its equal, if not the Continent. There has been spent in restoration on this porch alone a sum of nearly £3000. In the muniment room over this famous porch is still to be seen the old oak chests in which Chatterton asserted he found the MSS. of the Rowley poems.

Enter the main building, and take your stand near

Churches

the antique wrought-iron gates at the western extremity of the nave. On each side rise columns to support a roof which rivals in loveliness, loftiness, and lightness of design all other churches in England. The carving of the roof is full of elaborate detail; but, as it stretches over the head to the Lady Chapel, it seems a sheet in perspective of the richest embroidery. The clerestory windows admit a soft twilight, which falls on the groined arches sufficiently to bring out the light and shade of their masonry; while concealing half their beauty, the twilight lends them the majesty and mystery of shadow. Opening to the eye of the beholder is a bewildering wealth of beauty in the minute fluting, foliated tracery ribs and capitals, which enrich its glorious interior. Among its monumental effigies especially to be noted are those in the south aisle to the memory of William Canynge, the younger, and his wife, Joan; whilst the south transept finds yet another to him in priestly robes—for late in life he was ordained and became Dean of Westbury College—near which will be found a quaint effigy which is popularly supposed to be Canynge's almoner, and close by stands the memorial to the same worthy's cook, with the implements of his office incised on the memorial slab.

So great a merchant was Canynge in his lifetime that he had in his hands the chief trade with Northern Europe, and his transactions were on so large a scale in 1450, that when English trade was forbidden in virtue of a treaty with the King of Denmark, Canynge was specially exempted for his services to the Danes, and had therefore for a time the monopoly of their trade.

Bath and Bristol

To man his fleet of ten vessels he employed eight hundred seamen, to say nothing of the carpenters, masons, and other workmen engaged in the rebuilding his church of St. Mary Redcliffe. Five times he was Mayor of Bristol, and twice represented her in Parliament, retiring in his old age to Westbury College, where he became its Dean and there died. The chapel of his "great house" is still happily extant in Redcliffe Street, the main portion of the building having been destroyed by fire some thirty years ago.

Near Canynge's tomb there was originally an interesting epitaph as follows: "Here lies Thomas Chamber, of this parish, merchant, and his wife, Ann. She died 1620, he, October 1647—

> "When I was young, in wars I shed my blood
> Both for my Queen and for my country's good;
> In elder years my care was chief to be
> Soldier to Him who shed His blood for me."

Among interesting memorials that to Admiral Sir William Penn, the right hand of Blake when he fought the Dutch, and the father of the great colonizer, William Penn, who founded Pennsylvania, arrests the attention of the visitor. His monument, surmounted by his armour and tattered banners, will be found on the wall of the tower. He died in 1670.

À propos of which, after Blake's great victory over the Dutch in 1653, fifty prisoners were brought to Bristol and confined in the crypt of Redcliffe Church.

The rib of the Dun Cow, which according to the legend supplied all Bristol with milk, may still be seen

ST. MARY REDCLIFFE, LOOKING EAST

Churches

on the left of the western entrance to the church. This, however, is far more likely to have been a whale's rib brought home to Bristol in 1497 by John Cabot from Newfoundland.

In St. Mary Redcliffe, Whitefield preached his farewell sermon ere taking ship for Georgia "to such a congregation as my eyes never yet saw . . . multitudes followed me home weeping."

The friendship of a former vicar, the Rev. Thomas Broughton, with the composer of *The Messiah* is commemorated by the "Handel" window. Colston's memory, too, is preserved in the same manner. And only last January, Cabot, Canynge, and other fifteenth-century worthies were likewise honoured by the glazier's art. But the crowning association connected with this remarkable church is that of Chatterton, the boy poet. His uncle was its sexton, and doubtless through him Chatterton gained access to the old MSS. in the muniment room above the north porch, which formed the data that inspired his famous "Rowley Poems." Be that as it may, those poems are full of allusions to the church of his waking dreams, and permeated with the medieval atmosphere engendered by that stately house of prayer. Well might Dr. Johnson when visiting Redcliffe Church in 1776 exclaim : "This is the most extraordinary young man that has encountered my knowledge ; it is wonderful how the whelp has written such things." The travesty of a memorial to the most famous of Bristol's sons, at the north-east corner of Redcliffe Church, is an insult to his imperishable memory. Another famous literary association is the fact that the

Bath and Bristol

twin poets, Coleridge and Southey, were both married there in the closing months of 1795.

In connection with this famous church, there exists a charming custom of decorating the building and strewing it with rushes annually on Whitsunday. This custom is of considerable antiquity and dates back to the year 1494, when William Mede, a merchant of the city, who had been three times Mayor, gave property on the Welsh Back, the rent of which was to pay for an annual sermon on the feast of Pentecost before the Mayor and Commonalty of Bristol. For this the preacher was entitled to 6s. 8d., and the Mayor was enjoined to invite him to his table and give him a good dinner, for which the giver was allowed 3s. 4d., the residue was for strewing the church with flowers and rushes, ringing of bells, etc.

Temple Church

A church that enjoys a considerable repute is that of Temple, originally built by the Knights Templars, chiefly from the curious fact that its tower lies quite 4 feet out of the perpendicular—a local leaning tower of Pisa. The year 1145 is given as the date when the Knights began its erection, for the district south-east of the Avon had been granted them by their powerful friend, Robert, the great Earl of Gloucester.

The church, however, which they erected was small, and must not be identified with the present structure, which is of later date than its Norman original. The oldest portion of the existing building is the chancel, which belongs to the Decorated period. The roof of the

Churches

nave is pointed and divided into squares by oak ribs with bosses at the intersections. The tower as far as the trefoil band, situated two-thirds of its height, probably dates from the close of the fourteenth century. William Wycester, a trustworthy and contemporary authority, states that the tower was built anew in 1460, but this doubtless applies to the stage of the tower above the trefoil band referred to.

The deviation of the tower from the perpendicular is no doubt due to the marsh-like character of its foundation. In the year 1568 the Duke of Norfolk, subsequently beheaded, visited the church accompanied by the Earl of Worcester, Lord Berkeley, and others, out of curiosity to see the tower shake when the bells were rung. Braun in his *Theatrum Urbium* (1576) states that the tower had been torn from the body of the church leaving a great chink from the roof to the foundation, and says that Ortelius, the geographer, had put a stone of the size of a goose's egg in the chink when the bells were rung, and it was crushed to pieces. This noble tower, which was getting much decayed, has within the last year or two been thoroughly restored. In regard to the interior of the church, there is a stately impressiveness about it that strikes the beholder, doubtless due to the fact that the nave and aisles are unusually wide and lofty, being divided by arcades of tall arches the full height of the building, carried by remarkably slender and graceful pillars.

Among special objects of interest is the Weavers' Chapel or north aisle of the chancel, so named from the Guild of Weavers having anciently worshipped there.

Bath and Bristol

In the chancel is a monument to John Stone, thrice Mayor of Bristol, who died in 1575. On one occasion while he was at mass here in Bloody Mary's reign, there came one Richard Sharp, a weaver, out of a little door in the Weavers' Chapel (this doorway has been filled up, but its outline may be seen) and exclaimed, "Fie upon the idolatrous worship." Thereupon this John Stone caused him to be apprehended, and being convicted he was publicly burnt for the offence on St. Michael's Hill.

There are many objects of exceptional interest contained in this church, not forgetting its communion plate and furniture. A remarkable specimen of early metal work is the unique candelabrum of the fourteenth century, which is in the chancel, with its statuettes, St. George and the Dragon below, and the Blessed Virgin with the infant Jesus above — one of the most important examples of early English metal work extant. Curious to say, there is a copy of it at St. Michael's Mount, Cornwall, made in 1788. Note, too, the magnificent grills or screens of seventeenth-century wrought iron-work on either side of the chancel, which are of exceptional interest and rarity. There are also one or two brasses which should not be overlooked. One of these represents the half figure of a layman, with an interesting Latin inscription of which the following is a translation :—

"Thou art witness, O Christ, that this stone is not here laid to adorn the body, but to commemorate the spirit. You who pass by, whether old, middle-aged, or youth, make supplication for me, so that I may attain hope of pardon."

Among the church's personal associations will be

Churches

found that of Colston and Chatterton. Colston was baptized here, 8th November 1636. Chatterton was a personal friend of the then vicar, the Rev. Alexander Catcott, who was the only one in Bristol who truly estimated the boy's extraordinary mental ability. Unfortunately, he fell under the lash of Chatterton's satiric pen, which effectually put an end to their friendship. Among the church's treasures is a poem of Chatterton's, dealing with the Knights Templars. John Wesley, who was a friend of a later vicar, the Rev. Easterbrook, frequently preached there, and also conducted the marriage service on one occasion.

St. Mark's—The Lord Mayor's Chapel

To the noble family of the Berkeleys of Gloucestershire is due the foundation of this very beautiful chapel, part of a far larger building known as Gaunt's Hospital, for the accommodation of a hundred destitute or sick men. It was originally founded by Sir Maurice Berkeley de Gaunt, grandson of Robert Fitzharding, 1220 A.D.; aided by his successor, Robert de Gourney, and his younger brother, Sir Henry de Gaunt. These members of the great baronial family may be regarded as the joint founders.

In the year 1534 this building was surrendered to King Henry VIII, four hundred and twenty ounces of plate being included; later the whole of the buildings were acquired by the Corporation for the sum of £1000. The chapel was by them granted to the French Huguenots for worship, who remained in possession till

1721, when it was fitted up for the use of the Mayor and Corporation.

Situated opposite the Cathedral on the north-east side of College Green, in the midst of a setting of early Georgian houses, it presents with its pretty red sandstone tower an object of considerable interest. Entering by the west door a descent of several steps leads to the floor of the chapel, which measures 120 feet in length and 21 feet 6 inches in width.

Its architecture is considered to be mid-thirteenth century, a period when the Early English was merging into the Decorated. The mixture of styles here is well worthy of careful study. On the north and south sides of the chapel is a range of grotesque corbels belonging to the Early English building; some of the windows are of the same style, but of rather advanced design. The great west window, which occupies nearly the whole front, is of eight lights, and is a combination of the Decorated and Perpendicular styles. In the side aisle is "a subarctuated window of three lights rich with ball flower"; this is pure Decorated. The tower was finished in 1487. Graceful arches open into the transepts, that on the south formed by the lower storey of the tower. The naturalistic character of the foliage adorning the capitals of the responds indicates the beginning of the change in the style of architecture. The east end of the chapel with its fine altarpiece of late Perpendicular niches and tabernacle work, is stated to have been executed by Miles Salley, Bishop of Llandaff, whose tomb is conspicuous on the south side of the altar. He died about 1516. Particularly interesting is the Jesus' Chapel, otherwise the Poyntz Chapel, so

ST. MARY REDCLIFFE, FROM PRINCE'S WHARF

Churches

named after its founder, Sir Robert Poyntz of Iron Acton, which fills in the angle between the tower and sanctuary. This is the latest portion of the building, finished about 1520, and is one of the most beautiful examples of its period. It is roofed with a fan-vault which contains the arms of Henry VIII with those of Queen Catherine of Aragon, and has a series of beautiful niches round the walls. Its east window contains the only original, though not the only old glazing in the chapel, and its floor is unique in this country, being paved with Moorish tiles (azuleias) from Spain.

The chapel is fortunate in possessing a large amount of old glass, chiefly foreign. This is authoritatively stated to have been brought chiefly from Fonthill, Wilts, the home of the famous William Beckford.

Note the scourging of Christ in one of the south windows, which is remarkable for the use made of "sprinkled ruby" to represent His lacerated body. In the outer south aisle is a beautiful window containing a figure in pontificals to represent St. Thomas à Becket.

It is a copy of a painting by West, and was purchased from Fonthill Abbey; having previously cost Beckford 280 guineas. The old oak ceiling is a splendid example of ecclesiastical woodwork. It is divided in square compartments by deep moulded ribs, and at the points of intersection is enriched with gilt bosses, stars, spandrils, and corbels. Not unworthy of notice, too, is the aperture named Squint or Hagioscope, situated in the side aisle, which in the days of Roman Catholicism allowed a person there stationed to see the service at the High Altar.

Bath and Bristol

The picture enshrined in the tabernacle work of the reredos is the work of a local artist, John King, 1829, and represents the dead Christ surrounded by His sorrowing disciples.

The general effect of the chapel's interior is very impressive. The emblazoned roof, rich fretwork stalls of dark oak, carved tabernacles, the ancient tombs with their sculptured canopies and outstretched figures of churchmen and warriors, the sombre illumination derived from the traceried windows glowing with images of saints and martyrs ; all combine to enhance devotional feeling and sanctity in the minds of its worshippers.

Perhaps, however, the most remarkable feature of interest in this St. Mark's Chapel is its series of monuments of bygone worthies of the city, dating from the thirteenth century.

Among these, especially noteworthy are Miles Salley, Bishop of Llandaff's, recumbent effigy in full eucharistic vestments, with mitre and crozier, and that supposed to be to the memory of Sir Maurice Berkeley of Uley and his wife, 1464 A.D. Interesting, too, is the effigy of Lord Richard Berkeley, who died in 1604, if only for the curious admonition, which, translated, runs : " Though all men may desire to know my name and race, yet no man may desire to know my mind. If any should take up the inquiry who I am, reply, I know not ; but let me advise that man to know himself ! " In the south aisle chapel will be found the recumbent cross-legged effigies of Maurice de Gaunt and Robert de Gourney in chain armour, both of thirteenth century date, the original founders of the Hospital.

ST. STEPHEN'S CHURCH

Churches

St. Stephen's Church

Those who pass round the College Green on their way to the Tramways Centre must from time to time have been struck with the Venetian character of the scene—the Float with its shipping and boats in the foreground, and in the background, dominating the entire scene, the magnificent church tower of St. Stephen. The date of this church is uncertain, but it was evidently in existence prior to the fourteenth century, for as early as 1304 a legacy was left to the then rector. It originally belonged to the Abbots of Glastonbury, and was in their possession till the Dissolution. Between 1450 and 1490 it was entirely rebuilt, at the joint expense of Glastonbury Abbey and the parishioners, the tower being added by the munificence of one of Bristol's merchant princes named John Shipward, who was Mayor in 1455. "This tower," according to Freeman the historian, "is remarkable for having æsthetically dispensed with buttresses, those which it has having so slight a projection as hardly at all to influence the general effect. It has, indeed, almost the appearance of a Gothic version of the old Italian Campanile. However this may be, its idea, which is one quite peculiar to itself, though it may not altogether approve itself to our preconceived notions, must be allowed to be, in point of fact, magnificently worked out." Whatever theory may have governed its design, the result has triumphantly vindicated it, for as the tower ascends from stage to stage with increasing profusion of ornament, crowned finally with its diadem of latticed battlements and pinnacles, it presents by its

Bath and Bristol

impressive proportions one of the finest examples of English church towers. The interior of this church somewhat belies its stately exterior, inasmuch that there are no features of architectural adornment calling for especial notice. The nave and chancel are divided on each side from the north and south aisles by seven uniform and finely-proportioned moulded arches, supported by clustered columns, having capitals embellished with demi-angels holding unfolded scrolls. A rood-loft formerly separated the chancel from the nave. The roof is of oak, and strongly resembles that of the Lord Mayor's Chapel.

The south porch is interesting and striking by reason of its elaboration of ornament, especially the beautiful fan tracery of its roof. There is no wealth of monuments in the church, though one or two are well worthy of notice, more particularly that to the memory of Captain Martin Pring, the famous navigator and adventurer, with its quaint and elaborate epitaph. There is, too, at the end of the south aisle a sumptuous monument to the memory of Sir George Snigge, judge and recorder of Bristol from 1592 to 1604. In this church formerly existed seven chantries with endowments for singing masses to the souls of their founders. One of these was founded by Edward Blanket, erroneously credited with having invented that domestic article of comfort, the blanket. This church is honoured by being closely associated with the very important and wealthy Society known as the Merchant Venturers', to whose munificence the stained-glass window at the west end is due. Attached to it also is the Guild of St. Stephen's Ringers, which is of ancient origin. According to its Ordinances, they provide " that none

Churches

shall be of the said Society but those that shall be of honest, peaceable, and good conversation." A curious item is as follows: "If any one of the said Company shall be so rude as to run into the Belfry before he do kneel down and pray, as every good Christian ought to do, he shall pay, for the first offence, sixpence, and for the second he shall be cast out of the Company."

St. Peter's Church

This, the oldest of the city churches, is believed to have been the parish church of the old royal manor of Barton, and doubtless contemporary in construction with Bristol Castle, the barbican of which stood at the chancel end. During the Sieges of Bristol it was in imminent peril of being destroyed by the Cromwellian Governor, Nathaniel Fiennes; fortunately the arrival of Prince Rupert and his army prevented this wanton act of vandalism.

Little of the original church remains, for the present structure, apart from the tower, is of the fifteenth century. The massive proportions of the tower, the walls of which are said to be six feet thick, point conclusively to its Norman origin.

Though a large and airy church, it is not remarkable for architectural beauty, but it possesses several features of interest. It formerly possessed several fine brasses, but nearly all have disappeared. A very good one, however, still remains at the east end of the south aisle, representing a priest (Robert Loud) in vestments and bearing a chalice, dated 1461. A conspicuous tomb that attracts attention is that of Robert Aldworth and his wife, who resided in the magnificent half-timbered house adjoining, known as St. Peter's Hospital, considered one of the most striking examples of enriched timber building in England. This sumptuous tomb, with kneeling figures of Aldworth and his wife, is situated in the south aisle. Aldworth died in 1634. There, too, at the east end is a lofty canopied tomb of early Jacobean date and richly carved, commemorating Lady Newton of Barr's Court. From the middle aisle has disappeared a stone which bore the interesting inscription : " Sir John Cadaman, Knight, was beheaded in the Castle for killing Miles Callowhill, an officer of the garrison, while Prince Rupert had possession of Bristol, and was buried in this church the 9th of April 1645." In the south aisle was formerly a chantry dedicated to the honour of the " Blessed Mary of Bellhouse." In 1521 we find the mirror of all courtesy, the Duke of Buckingham, making his oblation there in the sum of 3s. 4d. There in its churchyard in a nameless grave lie the remains of Richard Savage the poet, whose *Life* by his friend Dr. Johnson has given him, we fear, undeserving fame. Being imprisoned for debt, his humane gaoler, Abel Dagge, showed him much kindness, and when he died of fever in 1743, bore a large share of the expense of his burial. Within recent years an inscribed stone to his memory has been placed in the south wall of the church.

St. James's Church

This church, originally a priory of the Benedictines, is situated on the north side of the city in The Barton, and

Churches

is dedicated to the Virgin Mary and St. James. It was built by Robert, Earl of Gloucester. This great Earl, when engaged in constructing the keep of the Castle of Bristol, is said to have devoted one-tenth of the stones which he had brought over from Normandy to the building of this priory. It was originally of considerable extent, but the church alone survives, and even this has suffered much by demolition and mutilation. The western façade is the only accessible portion of the exterior of the church of which the interesting character of the Norman building may be discerned. Above the doorway at this end is an arcade of interesting arches, three of which are pierced for circular-headed windows. Independently of the pointed arches formed by intersection, there are in this arcade other and very early examples of the same advanced style of arch. Over the arcade note the small but beautiful rose window. The ancient clerestory remains, but is exteriorly hidden on the north side by the adjoining houses, and on the south by the parapet of the aisle. The south clerestory, however, exhibits an interesting arcade extending the whole length of the outside of the church ; it consists of a series of shafts, with the common Norman capital supporting arches of irregular forms, some pointed, some elliptic, with semicircular ones over the windows : near the east remains one corbel, showing the height at which a corbel table once passed above these arches. In the north side the clerestory windows have what Bloxam calls nook-shafts, and are in other respects similar to those on the south ; but here there is no arcade to connect them.

Bath and Bristol

The tower is of the perpendicular style, and dates from the latter half of the fourteeth century, but since then has been considerably altered and repaired.

The nave is divided from the aisles by two rows of massive Norman piers, which are connected by semi-circular arches. The eastern end is a modern reproduction of the Norman style of building, and consists of three circular-headed windows with chevron mouldings, and beneath are two series of stone arcades.

This Priory of St. James stood outside the walls of the town northwards from the Castle, whose frowning towers and bastions grimly overlooked the monks pacing the grass-clad precincts telling their beads and muttering their aves.

This priory was a cell to the Abbey of Tewkesbury, and as early as the beginning of the fourteenth century, a population having gathered round it, the nave of the church, by grant of the Abbot, was assigned to the use of the parishioners, who were required to erect a square belfry or tower, and to cover or reconstruct the roof of the nave from the tower to the western gable. This latter demand led to friction between the Prior and the parishioners, which was healed by the parish paying an annual rent of forty-two pence derived from lands at Redland.

The church ceased to be a priory in the year 1540, the last Prior being allowed an annual pension of £13, 6s. 8d. during his lifetime. It was then granted, together with its lands, manor-house, etc., to Henry Brayne, a merchant of London, upon whose decease it passed to his son, and finally after successive ownerships to the Corporation of Bristol.

Churches

In the wall of the south aisle is a recessed tomb supporting a recumbent figure, purporting, according to the modern inscription, to represent Robert, the great Earl of Gloucester, the founder of St. James's Priory, who was buried within the walls of the church. This is confirmed by Leland, who states that " Robertus, consul Cownte of Gloucestershire, (was) buried in the *quiere*."

In an ancient chronicle of Tewkesbury, cited in Dugdale, it is mentioned that this illustrious Earl died in 1147, and his body was honourably interred in the choir of the Priory of St. James, Bristol.

Another famous personage here interred was the Princess Eleanor of Brittany, whose hapless life was one long imprisonment within the walls of the adjoining Castle, where four knights continually kept guard over her. Later, by order of King Henry III, her remains were disinterred and removed to Amesbury.

Connected with this church was a remarkable fair which existed for centuries and was famous throughout Europe, namely, St. James's Fair. Its origin appears to date from the thirteenth century, for Walter de Cantilupe, Bishop of Worcester, ordained (1238 A.D.) that a feast of relics should be yearly held in the Priory of St. James during the week of Pentecost, and that fifteen days' indulgence should be granted to all who visited the feast with their alms. This form of festal custom was later superseded by a business or fancy fair held during the first fortnight of September in each year, for in the year 1292 the Archbishop of Canterbury in his rules governing his household particularly mentions that " robes were to be bought at St. James's tide," namely, St. James's

Bath and Bristol

Fair. In the seventeenth century its fame, though centuries had elapsed, was still as great as ever, so much so, indeed, that ships bound thereto were the object of special attention by Turkish corsairs. As many as eleven sail of these, flying English colours, were on one occasion reported to be in the Channel waiting to seize passengers bound for Bristol. The Mayor of Penzance (4th July 1636) gave notice of this to the Secretary of State, complaining that His Majesty's fleet had not been seen off Cornwall for fourteen days, and that the Turkish corsairs intended to be about the Lizard Point and Land's End against St. James's Fair.

This fair lasted well into the nineteenth century, but ere its abolishment it had sadly declined from its ancient importance as the market-place of Europe, and had become the great rendezvous of showmen, circuses, acrobats, sweet and fancy booths, and other and more questionable forms of allurement to the many-headed beast. At this fair there might have been seen at one time Belzoni, afterwards the famous Egyptian explorer, who was accustomed there to exhibit his herculean feats of strength and skill.

In St. James's Churchyard are interred some of Charles Wesley's children. He lived for over twenty years in Charles Street in this parish. A tablet marks the house.

St. John the Baptist

Beyond the very interesting fact that the present church is built on the old city wall, under the tower of which the only ancient gateway of the city still exists,

Churches

there is little to record. The church is a simple rectangle, undivided by aisles, but the nave is separated from the chancel by a tall pointed arch, which is the principal relieving feature of the edifice.

In the north window of the chancel is a delicately-wrought episcopal mitre in stained glass, once in the possession of Wells Cathedral. In the vestry, too, is an old hour-glass, a most curious relic of other days, and is, with its stand, in excellent preservation. In the middle aisle of this church are two brasses denoting that Thomas Rowley, merchant and sheriff, died January 1478, and Margaret, his wife, died 1470. The name Rowley is quite likely to have come under the notice of Chatterton, and hence his adoption of it as a cover to his poetic fictions that puzzled the learned world for so long. At the gateway of St. John's great Elizabeth halted when visiting Bristol in 1574, and was welcomed by three boys representing Salutation, Gratulation, and Obedient Good Will.

We strongly suspect that Her Majesty was hard put to in listening patiently to the fulsome and long-drawn-out hexameters they uttered in her praise. It was the ringing of the bell of this church which was, in the Sieges of Bristol, to be the signal for the admittance into the city of Prince Rupert and his followers. The conspiracy, however, failed, with deadly consequences to its prime movers, Messrs. Yeoman and Boucher.

CHAPTER VII

BRISTOL'S CONNECTION WITH LITERATURE

LONDON and Edinburgh excepted, there is no great city in the British Isles more closely associated with our country's most glorious heritage—its literature. Famous indeed are those who have been thus associated. One of the first names in Bristol's hierarchy of letters is that of William Langland, the great contemporary of the Father of English poetry, Chaucer, for it was during the former's stay in Bristol that he wrote his "Richard the Redeless."

Nor must we forget that their immediate successor, John Lydgate, enshrined Bristol in his famous poem, "The Child of Bristol." This interesting poem finds an honoured place among the Camden Society's publications.

In Bristol, too, was born in 1415 that old-world itinerant and man of letters, William Wycestre (whose family name was Botoner). He did an invaluable work for his native city by recording so lovingly and minutely its topographical details, that enables us of the twentieth century to picture Bristol as she appeared in the fifteenth. It is recorded of him by a contemporary that when past forty years of age "he hath goon to scole to a Lumbard, called Karoll Giles, to lern and

Bristol's Connection with Literature

to be red in Poetre or els in Frensh; for he hath byn with the same Karoll every day ii times or iii, and hath bought divers boks of hym, for the which (as I suppose) he hath put hymself in danger" (*i.e.* in debt) "to the same Karoll. . . . And he said that he wold be as glad and as fayn of a gode boke of Frensh or of Poetre (as some would be) to purchase a fair manior." A disciple indeed of Chaucer's famous scholar, "The Clerke of Oxenford," was this old-world bookman, for we learn that on one occasion he rode to Shirehampton and inquired of Thomas Young there respecting "a great book of ethics" and "The Myrrour of Dames," which he had evidently lent him. There his host received him with "a cheerful countenance, and his wife welcomed me." That the torch of learning was kept brightly burning in Bristol in those far-off days is shown by the fact that the famous Greek scholar, Grocyn, who was the first to teach that language at Oxford, was brought up and educated in this western city.

A famous printer and publisher was born here in 1527, named William Norton. His name appears among the original freemen of the Stationers' Company in their charter granted by Mary and Philip in 1555, and he was several times elected its Master. Another famous sixteenth-century literary worthy was also born in Bristol—John Fowler, the celebrated Catholic scholar. So learned was he that old Anthony Wood, the Oxford historian, tells us "that he might have passed for another Robert or Henry Stephens." St. George's parish, in the east of the city, had the honour of giving birth in 1563 to Sir John Stradling, one of the most celebrated

Bath and Bristol

men of his time. So great, indeed, were his scholastic attainments that he was considered "a miracle for his forwardness in learning." William Camden eagerly cultivated his friendship, and quotes him in his famous work, *Britannia*, edition 1607.

In the following century (the seventeenth) two world-famous Diarists visited Bristol—John Evelyn and Samuel Pepys, both of whom were much struck with Bristol and recorded their impressions. Evelyn, who came in 1654, was so surprised at its magnitude that he compared it to London "in its manner of building."

Pepys, who came fourteen years later, in 1668, confirmed Evelyn's opinion by saying, " walked with my wife and people through the city, which is in every respect another London, that one can hardly know it stands in the country." His maid " Deb." (who was a Bristolian) " going to see her Uncle Butts, and leaving my wife with the mistress of the place, I to see the Key, which is a large and noble place ; and to see the new ship building by Bally " (Baylie). " It will be a fine ship, and walked back to the Sun, where I find Deb. come back, and with her, her Uncle, a sober merchant, very good company, and so like one of our sober wealthy London merchants, as pleased me mightily. Here we dined, and much good talk with me, 7s. 6d. Then walked with Butts and my wife and company round the Key, and he showed me the Custom House, and made me understand many things of the place, and led me through Marsh Street where our girl " (Deb.) " was born. But Lord ! the joy that was among the old people of the place, to see Mrs. Willet's daughter, it seems her mother being a brave woman and

THE "MENAPIA", AN IRISH TRADER
(ST. STEPHEN'S CHURCH IN THE BACKGROUND)

Bristol's Connection with Literature

mightily beloved! And so brought us back by surprise to his house, where a substantial good house and well furnished; and did give us good entertainment of strawberries, a whole venison pasty, and plenty of brave wine, and above all Bristol Milk : where comes in another poor woman, who, hearing that Deb. was here, did come running hither, and with her eyes so full of tears, and her heart so full of joy, that she could not speak when she came in, that it made me weep too : I protest I was not able to speak to her, which I would have done, to have diverted her tears. Butt's wife a good woman, and so sober and substantial as I was never more pleased anywhere. So thence took leave, and he with us through the City. He showed us the place where the merchants meet here, and a fine cross yet standing like Cheapside" (it stood at the junction of the four principal streets, Wine Street, Corn Street, etc.). "And so . . . by moonshine to Bath again, about ten o'clock."

Linked with Bristol, too, is that famous essayist and hymn-writer of the seventeenth century, Joseph Addison. Dr. Goulston, Bishop of Bristol, was his uncle, and it is a tradition that he wrote some of his *Spectator* papers here at Brislington. In 1718 he came to take the Hotwells waters, and writing to his friend Swift he remarks : " The greatest pleasure I have met with for months is the conversation of my old friend Dr. Smalridge, who is to me the most candid and agreeable of bishops."

A brief chapter in the life of David Hume, the historian and philosopher, was enacted in Bristol, where for a short time in 1734 he was a clerk in the employ

Bath and Bristol

of Michael Miller, a merchant residing at 16 Queen Square (the house is still standing).

He very soon found the irksomeness of his position, and his having had the temerity to correct his employer's English hastened his departure. "I tell you what, Mr. Hume," said the irate and successful merchant, "I have made £20,000 by my English, and I won't have it mended."

In November of 1739 we find that his distinguished contemporary, Alexander Pope the poet, was on a visit to the Hotwells, and was greatly impressed with the appearance of the city. Writing to his friend Mrs. Blount, he refers to the "twenty odd pyramids smoking over the town" (the glasshouses). "Then you come first to the old walls (Temple Gate) and over a bridge, built on both sides like London Bridge, and as much crowded, with a strange mixture of seamen, women, children, loaded horses, asses, and sledges with goods, dragging along all together without posts to separate them. From thence you come to the Key along the old wall, with houses on both sides, and in the middle of the street, as far as you can see, hundreds of ships, their masts as thick as they can stand by one another, which is the oddest and most surprising sight imaginable. This street is fuller of them than the Thames from London Bridge to Deptford. . . .

"The streets are as crowded as London; but the best image I can give of it is, 'tis as if Wapping and Southwark were ten times as big, or all their people ran into London."

At a later date he again paid Bristol a visit.

Bristol's Connection with Literature

Associated with the city, too, at this period was Richard Savage the poet, whose name will go down the stream of time with that of his great friend Dr. Johnson, who wrote his *Life* and thus secured him a permanent niche in the temple of fame that his own merits unfortunately do not entitle him. For the sordid, shiftless, ungrateful career he led and his insolent demands for money disgusted every one with whom he was on terms of friendship. Though treated with great marks of favour by the leading merchants of Bristol and invited to their homes and public feasts, all the kindness showered upon him was recklessly abused, till at last, wearied out with his base ingratitude, further help was refused; he then revenged himself by a satire that is best described by the adjective his name implies.

But the supreme poet whose connection with Bristol is and ever will be its greatest literary glory, is the absolutely miraculous Chatterton, "the sleepless soul that perished in his pride." The more his all too brief life, ending in his eighteenth year, is studied, the more shall we realize that he was indeed of imagination all compact. Well might Dr. Johnson exclaim when visiting Bristol in 1776 : "This is the most extraordinary young man that has encountered my knowledge ; it is wonderful how the whelp has written such things." In the heirarchy of England's poets, considering his youth, he has no peer save Keats, and even he, if judged by the work he had created at the age when Chatterton died, would have to yield the pride of place. What Keats himself thought of Chatterton is eloquently expressed by the dedication to his maiden poem "Endymion" : "Inscribed

Bath and Bristol

with every feeling of pride and regret to the memory of the most English of poets except Shakespeare—Thomas Chatterton."

Two dominating characteristics were embodied in Chatterton, the first of which was that, like Blake, he was a dreamer of dreams, to such a degree that it is hard to say which had the greatest influence upon him, the dream life or the real life; the other, that "damned native, unconquerable pride" which in the end destroyed him. There have been few poets in the world's history whose creative imagination has burned at a whiter heat than Chatterton's. You may turn over page after page of his Rowley cycle of poems without coming across an inane line, for they are lit up by flashes of lyrical beauty and intensity of imaginative power. Like Shelley's lark—

> "And soaring ever singest,
> And singing still doth soar."

Chatterton in his communion with nature is also fully entitled to divide with Burns and Cowper the honour of heralding in a nobler and truer era of English poetry, the culminating point of which produced that epoch-making volume, the *Lyrical Ballads* of Wordsworth and Coleridge, in 1798.

The pivot round which the whole life of Chatterton revolved was Redcliffe Church, for that architectural dream in stone permeates with its medieval atmosphere the best of his work.

Beneath the shadow of this magnificent edifice he was born in the School-house (happily still preserved), Pile

Bristol's Connection with Literature

Street, on the 20th November 1752, the son of a schoolmaster and sub-chanter in Bristol Cathedral, his posthumous birth occurring little more than three months after his father's death. From his earliest years the church of St. Mary Redcliffe possessed for him a singular fascination. Indeed, he was never happier than when within its walls or precincts. But the one place above all others that drew him like a charm was the muniment room. Long before he became a scholar at Colston's School on St. Augustine's Back (Colston Hall stands on its site), he had read and re-read the ancient MSS. which were stored in the old oak chests there. Here with their assistance he wrote his famous Rowley Poems, which he passed off on a credulous world as the work of a fifteenth-century monk. For eighty years after his death a mighty controversy raged among critics and antiquaries as to whether Rowley or Chatterton wrote them.

At the age of five Chatterton was sent by his widowed mother to the Pile Street School under her late husband's successor, but the latter could make nothing of him, and at length, his patience being exhausted by Chatterton's dullness, he sent him home as being too stupid to be taught. His mother was much grieved at this, and tried in vain to teach him herself. Indeed, so wanting in intelligence did he seem, that she despaired even of teaching him his letters, and at length began to think him an absolute fool, nor hesitated to tell him so.

During his seventh year, however, she chanced to show him an old musical MS. in French with illuminated capitals. This so fascinated him that, to use her own words, he "fell in love with it." From this MS. he

Bath and Bristol

learnt the alphabet, and progressed so rapidly that he was soon able to read from an old black-letter Testament. The torpidity of his mental powers now vanished, and henceforth his progress was as quick as before it had been slow. At seven, to his mother's surprise and joy, distinct improvement had taken place, and a year later he was so hungry for knowledge that he devoured every book he could lay his hands upon.

Even at this early stage of his life he already showed a masterful disposition and a desire for fame, for a friend of the family wishing to present him with a piece of china asked him what should be painted on it. He replied, "Paint me an angel with wings and a trumpet to trumpet my name over the world."

In 1760, when nearly eight years of age, he obtained entrance into the Colston School through the influence of the then vicar of Henbury. The dull monotony of the studies suited to those intended for commercial pursuits soon, however, proved distasteful, and he became wearied and disgusted.

His thirst, however, for reading was unabated, and most of his small amount of pocket-money went in the hire of books. Leaving the school in July 1767, he was apprenticed to John Lambert, attorney, 37 Corn Street, opposite the Exchange (since demolished). His apprenticeship indentures with other rare MSS., including the extraordinary Will, are among the literary treasures of the Civic Art Gallery.

Though the office hours were long his duties were light, consequently in his leisure or spare time he devoted himself most strenuously to self-improving studies and

BRISTOL BRIDGE

Bristol's Connection with Literature

poetical composition. His researches covered a wide field, embracing heraldry, metaphysics, astronomy, music, antiquities, medicine, and mathematics.

His first appearance in print was a fabricated antique account of the Mayor of Bristol passing over old Bristol Bridge in the year 1248. This composition appeared in *Felix Farley's Bristol Journal* on 1st October 1768, and created quite a stir in the city. About this period, too, Chatterton made the acquaintance of George Catcott and Henry Burgum, who were partners in a pewtering business at No. 2 Bristol Bridge.

Catcott, who was a fussy, self-important, and eccentric man, destitute of common sense, but possessed of extraordinary credulity, greedily swallowed all that Chatterton told him *re* the Rowley Poems alleged to have been found in the old chests in the muniment room, Redcliffe Church. His pompous and vain partner, Henry Burgum, was equally credulous; to him, therefore, Chatterton imparted the information that among the Rowleian MSS. was a document having the armorial bearings of the De Berghams, with proof of their descent from the time of the Conqueror. The native vanity of Burgum was aroused, and highly pleased with the news, he rewarded his informant with the sum of five shillings:—

> "What would Burgum give to get a name
> And snatch his blundering dialect from shame!
> What would he give to hand his memory down
> To Time's remotest boundary? A crown!"

Later Chatterton supplied him from the same source with his pedigree down to the year 1685, and with a

Bath and Bristol

poem alleged to have been written by one of his ancestors, John de Bergham, in 1320. These were rewarded with another crown.

Encouraged by his successful imposture, and having in the meantime been introduced to Catcott's brother, the Rev. Alexander Catcott, vicar of Temple Church, and to William Barrett, then projecting his well-known *History of Bristol*, he began bringing the latter various documents bearing on that subject, which were eagerly received without the slightest suspicion or attempt to test their genuineness. Needless to say, their inclusion in his *History* has seriously discredited that work.

About this time, yearning for recognition outside the city of his birth, he addressed himself to Horace Walpole, hoping to find in the Strawberry Hill dilettante a possible patron and friend to his muse.

Therefore, à propos of the latter's recently published work, *Anecdotes of Painting*, Chatterton forwarded him the following letter, enclosing Rowley's "Ryse of Peyncteynge in Englande," and some verses about Richard 1 :—

"BRISTOL, *March* 25, 1769, CORN STREET.

"SIR,—Being versed a little in antiquitys I have met with several curious manuscripts, among which the following may be of Service to you in any future edition of your truly entertaining *Anecdotes of Painting*. In correcting the mistakes (if any) in the Notes you will greatly oblige, your most humble servant,

"THOMAS CHATTERTON."

This letter was most promptly and courteously answered by Walpole. Thus encouraged, Chatterton

Bristol's Connection with Literature

posted off another batch of MSS., including the "Historie of Peyncters in Englande," with the frank admission that their sender, though a lover of literature, was in humble circumstances. These having been submitted by Walpole to his friends Gray and Mason, were pronounced to be forgeries. Naturally irritated, he wrote a letter which stung the proud and sensitive boy poet to the quick, and in so doing omitted to enclose the MSS. Chatterton had sent.

After repeated applications for their return, Chatterton, on 24th July, wrote Walpole the following proudly reproachful letter :—

"SIR,—I cannot reconcile your behaviour with the notions I once entertained of you. I think myself injured, Sir, and did you not know my circumstances, you would not dare to treat me thus.

"I have sent twice for a copy of the manuscripts—no ainswer from you. An explanation or excuse for your slence would oblige   THOMAS CHATTERTON."

This note produced the immediate return of the MSS., and effectually prevented further correspondence between them.

A pen portrait (for none other exists) describes Chatterton as being "well grown and manly, having a proud and stately bearing, his eyes grey and exceedingly brilliant." Barrett, who of course knew him well, said "he never saw such eyes—fire rolling at the bottom of them."

In regard to his Rowley Poems, read as examples of his wondrous poetic and lyrical power, the martial and

Bath and Bristol

magnificent chorus on Liberty with which the "Tragedy of Goddwyn" ends; and surely the exquisite dirge from his masterpiece "Ælla" is not unworthy of Shakespeare himself. None but a poet who anticipated Wordsworth in his love of nature could have written—

> "The budding floweret blushes at the light,
> The meads are sprinkled with the yellow hue;
> In daisied mantles is the mountain dight,
> The nesh young cowslip bendeth with the dew;
> The trees enleafèd, unto heaven straught,
> When gentle winds do blow, to whistling din are brought."

Sir Walter Scott, who reviewed his poems over a century ago, was particularly struck with the truth and fidelity to nature of the following stanzas:—

> "The sun was gleaming in the midst of day,
> Dead still the air, and eke the welkin blue,
> When from the sea arose in drear array
> A heap of clouds of sable sullen hue
> The which full fast unto the woodland drew,
> Hiding at once the sunne's festive face
> And the black tempest swelled and gathered up apace. . . .
>
> The gathered storm is ripe; the big drops fall;
> The sun-burnt meadows smoke and drink the rain;
> The coming ghastness doth the cattle pall
> And the full flocks are driving o'er the plain;
> Dashed from the clouds the waters sweep again;
> The welkin opes; the yellow lightning flies;
> And the hot fiery steam in mighty wreathings dies."

And let it be said with full consciousness of the great balladists of our language, there are few, considering its length, to surpass his noble and beautiful "Balade of Charitie."

Bristol's Connection with Literature

As to the Rowley Poems, it has often been asserted that they are forgeries—a term which implies the counterfeiting of work already in existence. But Chatterton did no such thing: he simply fathered off on a non-existent monk of the fifteenth century the creations of his own wonderful imagination. Unlike the common forger, his work in that direction has injured no one but himself. When we view all the circumstances of his all too brief and sordid life, the sterile age in which he lived with its false love of the antique, and his surprising mental acuteness, we are not at all surprised that he selected that path to the recognition of the world for which he so ardently longed, to issuing his poems as the work of a poor charity schoolboy.

Chatterton, too, was most unfortunate in his personal environment: the only one of his Bristol friends or acquaintances who truly gauged his remarkable powers was the Rev. Alexander Catcott, who said "he was capable of writing anything attributed to Rowley, and that he was, on the whole, the most extraordinary genius he had ever met with." But such was Chatterton's love of satirical composition that even he did not escape castigation at his hands, with a consequent breaking off of friendly intercourse. The solitary exception who escaped Chatterton's satiric pen was Michael Clayfield, distiller of Castle Street, to whom he had been introduced during the closing months of 1769. To this worthy man he was indebted for the loan of many works, and from these acquired the scientific knowledge which enabled him to write his fine poem, "The Copernican System," which appeared in the *Town and Country Magazine*, 1769,

Bath and Bristol

in which many of his poems had appeared. In that magazine was inserted his "Elegy on Thomas Phillips," the assistant master at Colston's School, from whom he had received much kindness.

About this time, sick with disappointed hopes and goaded to desperation by the galling and irksomeness of his uncongenial employment, he wrote to Clayfield that he intended putting an end to his life. Lambert, his employer, happened to see the letter, and at once brought it to the notice of Barrett, who interviewed Chatterton and so earnestly pointed out the folly and wickedness of such an act, that Chatterton was moved to tears. However, shortly after, doubtless as a means of quitting his distasteful employment, Lambert found, to his intense astonishment, the "Last Will and Testament of Thomas Chatterton" conspicuously placed on the boy's desk, which commenced with the words: "All this wrote between eleven and two o'clock on Saturday, in the utmost distress of mind, 14th April 1770":—

"This is the last Will and Testament of me, Thomas Chatterton, of the City of Bristol: being sound in Body, or it is the fault of my last surgeon. The soundness of my Mind the Coroner and Jury are to be the Judges of; desiring them to take notice, that the most perfect Masters of Human Nature in Bristol distinguish me by the Title of the Mad Genius. Therefore if I do a mad action, it is conformable to every action of my life, which all savored of insanity. . . ."

After reading this remarkable document, Lambert at once cancelled his indentures.

Bristol's Connection with Literature

Among his few friends a subscription was raised which fell short of £5, and with this slender capital he started by coach a few days later to take the great world of London by storm.

During the following four months he wrote for eleven journals there; for his industry, application, and fecundity were simply astounding. So remarkable was his facility of composition that his "Exhibition," which contains nearly 500 lines, was written in three days. Political squibs, songs, letters—in some of which to the *Middlesex Journal* he tried to rival Junius—flowed like water from his untiring pen, among his correspondents at this time being Lord Mayor Beckford, whom he interviewed.

Despite his untiring efforts and his amazing literary output, little substantial recognition was meted out to him, and he began to lose hope. Was it any wonder, when we consider the princely payment he received, even when his work was accepted? From the *Town and Country Magazine*, for sixteen songs, he received 10s. 6d.; for "The Consuliad," consisting of 250 lines, a like sum; for his magnificent "Balade of Charitie"—the last of the Rowley cycle—the doom of rejection. The only transient gleam of success came from his "The Revenge." For this he received five guineas, on the strength of which he sent a box of presents to his mother and sister.

This, however, was followed by the blackness of despair as disappointment succeeded disappointment. Infinitely pathetic is the picture of this, one of the world's greatest geniuses, eating his heart out with longing for the recognition that never came, and actually starving; too proud indeed to beg, and too honest to steal.

Bath and Bristol

Alas, poor Chatterton! On one occasion only his pride was overborne, and he was induced to accept some oysters; these he was observed to eat *ravenously*. Three days later Mrs. Angel, his landlady, feeling assured that the unhappy boy was literally starving, begged him, on 24th August, to take dinner with her; but his indomitable pride conquered his natural craving for food, and he assured her he was not hungry.

That very night, goaded to desperation, he perished by his own hand. Truly his eagle soul had beat itself to death against the pitiless bars of circumstance. There in the garret he was found next morning, his lifeless hand limply pointing to where, on the floor beneath, lay the phial that held the fatal draught of arsenic, and the countless fragments that strewed the floor, all that remained of his latest composition.

Not for him the Poets' Corner of Westminster Abbey, but the interment of a common pauper in the burial-ground of Shoe Lane Workhouse, long since swept away and built over. Yet though scorned, neglected, and starved in his life, Time, that brings its revenges, has produced glorious tributes to his imperishable genius. Wordsworth, Coleridge, Southey, Scott, Moore, and Campbell have been unanimous in their praise of his marvellous powers. To him Coleridge dedicated his *Monody*, Keats his *Endymion*, whilst Rossetti, in addition to inditing to his honour one of his noblest sonnets, wrote of him as "the absolutely miraculous Chatterton." Theodore Watts-Dunton says: "It seems impossible to refuse to Chatterton the place of the father of the new romantic school. As to the romantic spirit it would be

AUTUMN AT FRENCHAY

Bristol's Connection with Literature

difficult to name any one of his successors in whom the high temper of romance has shown so intense a life." As Dr. Richard Garnett says: "All recognise in him the most extraordinary literary phenomenon that the world ever saw."

Those interested in Chatterton will be glad to know that the most complete collection of MSS. relating to this remarkable genius is to be seen at the Bristol Civic Art Gallery. There will be found his extraordinary "Will," his poems "The Death of Sir Charles Bawdin," "Kew Gardens," the Bergham Arms and Pedigree; to say nothing of that priceless relic, the actual pocket-book in Chatterton's possession at the time of his death, containing entries recording his financial transactions with the various journals to which he contributed, by which we find there was actually due to him the sum of £10, 17s. 6d., a tithe of which would have averted his tragic fate.

To a Bristol bookseller, one Joseph Cottle, the world of literature owes a deep and lasting debt of gratitude for his generous aid and encouragement to that famous group of young men who were so closely associated with Bristol in the closing years of the eighteenth century. Remarkable indeed is the fact that a provincial bookseller had the undying honour of introducing to the world the first printed productions in volume form of such modern classics as Coleridge, Wordsworth, Lamb, and Southey.

It was through the medium of their mutual friend, Robert Lovell, the young Quaker poet, that Cottle was

Bath and Bristol

brought into touch with Coleridge and Southey, who at that time were busy formulating the great Pantisocratic scheme that was to take shape in the backwoods of America. These Utopian colonists were to consist of twelve gentlemen and twelve ladies of good education and liberal principles. The labour of each man for two or three hours a day, it was imagined, would suffice to support the colony — the produce to be common property. There was to be a good library, and ample leisure was to be devoted to study, discussion, and the education of the children, etc. But there was a fatal proviso in the scheme that speedily sealed its fate: " Every gentleman was to provide a sum of £125."

Coleridge and Southey had made each other's acquaintance at Oxford, for we find Southey writing to his friend, Grosvenor Bedford, on 12th June 1794, in reference to Coleridge: " He is of the most uncommon merit,—of the strongest genius, the clearest judgment, the best heart. My friend he already is, and must hereafter be yours."

One of the recreations of these Pantisocrats in Bristol was the joint production of the drama *The Fall of Robespierre*, two-thirds of which was written by Southey.

Cottle on his first meeting Southey was deeply impressed, and records: " Never will the impression be effaced, produced on me by this young man. Tall, dignified, possessing great suavity of manners; an eye piercing, with a countenance full of genius, kindliness, and intelligence, I gave him at once the right hand of fellowship, and to the moment of his decease that

Bristol's Connection with Literature

cordiality was never withdrawn." The house in which Southey was born, No. 9 Wine Street, has unfortunately just been pulled down (1914).

Cottle was also struck with Coleridge's appearance when they were introduced: "I instantly descried his intellectual character; exhibiting as he did, an eye, a brow, and a forehead, indicative of commanding genius."

Encouraged by his interest and sympathy, the poets submitted their early poems to the worthy Cottle, who not only read and admired them, but gave practical proof of his admiration by offering them generous terms for the copyright. As the two poets were on the eve of being married to the sisters Fricker, whose widowed mother resided at Redcliffe Hill, the offer was most opportune. Both were agreeably surprised at the generosity of Cottle, who offered them thirty guineas each for their poems. Not only so, but he promised Southey fifty for his projected *Joan of Arc*, and Coleridge a guinea and a half for every hundred lines he should write. The fact that Cottle essayed to be a poet himself may partly account for his generosity, though we fear his *Alfred* and *The Fall of Cambria* are poor passports to fame. His brother Amos also wrote verse, and both have been lashed by the whip of satire. Byron, in his *English Bards and Scotch Reviewers*, alludes to the latter in the following couplet:—

"Oh, Amos Cottle! Phœbus! what a name
To fill the speaking trump of fame."

Whilst Joseph figures in the lines ascribed to Canning—

"Cottle, not he by *Alfred* made famous,
But Joseph of Bristol, the brother of Amos."

Bath and Bristol

It will doubtless be noticed that in the latter couplet Canning has mixed up the identities of the brothers Cottle.

In the meantime, while preparing their poems for publication and awaiting converts to their great Pantisocratic scheme, Coleridge and Southey took lodgings in College Street, College Green—a tablet marks Coleridge's association with the house—and gave themselves up to dreams of philosophy and poetry. Alas! the realities of life soon disturbed them, and funds running low, the aid of Cottle was invoked, with the result that he lent them £5 to defray their lodging bill.

Turning about for means of income, they resolved on giving courses of lectures—Southey on history, and Coleridge on politics and morals. Both courses were well attended despite the unpopular opinions of the young orators.

On 4th October 1795, Coleridge was married at St. Mary Redcliffe Church, and he and his bride departed to spend their honeymoon at Clevedon (famous for its associations with the Hallams, Tennyson, Thackeray, etc.). But the newly wedded pair had been there but a few brief days ere the indispensable Cottle's help was sought to supply them with the following quaint assortment of household necessities: "A riddle slice; a candle box; two ventilators; two glasses for the wash-stand; one tin dust-pan; one small tin-kettle; one pair of candlesticks; one carpet brush; one flour dredge; three tin extinguishers; two mats; a pair of slippers; a cheese toaster; two large tin spoons; a Bible; a keg of porter; coffee; raisins; currants; catsup; nutmegs; allspice; cinnamon; rice; ginger;

Bristol's Connection with Literature

and mace "—to which the thoughtful Cottle added a piece of carpet.

About a month later (November 14th) Robert Southey led Edith Fricker, to whom he had long been engaged, to the altar at the same church. But it was Cottle's generosity that found the money for the wedding ring and licence, an act of true kindness that Southey remembered to the day of his death, and nobly acknowledged when at the height of his fame in a letter that does honour to the sterling manliness of its writer.

Meanwhile Coleridge had found out the very real inconvenience of being in so secluded a spot as Clevedon then was, deprived of the intellectual companionship of his Bristol friends and the books he was wont to browse upon at the Bristol Library in King Street. Consequently at the beginning of December he and his wife returned to Bristol and took rooms on Redcliffe Hill. What he thought of Clevedon and his regret on leaving it, will be found not the least interesting among his poems. No sooner had he returned to Bristol than with the enthusiasm of inexperience he embarked on his short-lived but famous magazine, *The Watchman*.

Armed with unbounded enthusiasm and an eloquently persuasive tongue, Coleridge started off in the following January on his *Watchman* tour, and succeeded in obtaining a thousand subscribers to support the magazine — a vivid account of which will be found in his *Biographia*. The first number appeared on March 1st, 1796; but, alas! its chief characteristic, from the waiting subscribers' point of view, was its deadly dullness (the unforgivable literary sin).

It lingered on, offending numbers of its subscribers by its heretical opinions, until No. 10 was reached, when it came to a close—an event not unforeseen by Coleridge's shrewd and trusty friend Thomas Poole, of Nether Stowey.

The despondency induced by the non-success of *The Watchman* was greatly alleviated by the timely and delicate generosity of the worthy Poole, who not only sent him money, but invited him to Nether Stowey to recruit. This kindly offer Coleridge gladly accepted, and spent a restful fortnight there.

Soon after his return to Bristol, early in April, Coleridge's first book of poems was published, entitled " *Poems on Various Subjects*, by S. T. Coleridge, late of Jesus College, Cambridge, 1796." Added interest in the volume is derived from the fact that it contains four sonnets by Charles Lamb. A copy of this rare little volume is in the Bristol Library, presented by the author. This, the first-fruits of his genius, numbers among them his " Monody on Chatterton."

In the June following Coleridge received the splendid offer — through the influence of the celebrated Dr. Beddoes of Clifton—which had it been accepted would have placed him in the proud position of independence for the rest of his life—the assistant editorship of the *Morning Chronicle*. But it was not to be : that fatal infirmity of indecision—his marked characteristic through life, barred his acceptance of it. Cursed with an irresolute will, life, that should have been full of splendid

Bristol's Connection with Literature

possibilities and a radiating centre of happiness to his family and friends, was clouded with unfulfilled hopes and financial embarrassment.

Later in this year of 1796, the Coleridges removed to Oxford Street, Kingsdown, and whilst the poet was absent at Birmingham on a visit to Charles Lloyd (whose acquaintance he had made on his *Watchman* tour), he received the pleasing intelligence of the birth of his first-born, Hartley.

This interesting event occurred on September 19th, 1796. The poet's joy expressed itself in three sonnets, one of which ended with that exquisite " touch of nature that makes the whole world kin "—

> " So for the Mother's sake the Child was dear,
> And dearer was the Mother for the Child."

Hastening back to Bristol, Coleridge was accompanied by Lloyd, whom he had fascinated with his eloquent conversation, and who had begged to be allowed to "domesticate" with him as a paying guest. Writing to Poole at a later date, Coleridge says : " Charles Lloyd wins upon me hourly ; his heart is uncommonly pure. . . . His joy and gratitude to Heaven for the circumstance of his domestication with me I can scarcely describe to you. . . ."

It was soon after this that the Coleridges and Lloyd migrated to Nether Stowey on a visit to Poole, due to the poet having conceived a passion for rural delights, despite his friends pointing out the folly of burying himself in so obscure a village, far from libraries and the mental stimulus of intellectual society.

Bath and Bristol

In the meantime, Southey, who had been on a visit to his uncle in Portugal, and having in vain applied himself to the study of law in London, and subsequently staying with friends at Norwich and Christchurch, had once more returned to the city of his birth, and settled at Westbury across the Downs. There he enjoyed, he tells us, " twelve happy months " in pursuit of the passion of his life—literary composition. " I never before or since," he says, " produced so much poetry in the same space of time." It was during his stay at Westbury that Southey projected his *Annual Anthology* for the year 1799–1800, which contains contributions from Coleridge, Lamb, Lloyd, Dyer, the brothers Cottle, Mrs. Robinson (Perdita), and Mrs. Opie.

Unfortunately, this prolific and pleasant period of his life was summarily cut short, for Southey's landlord desired re-possession, and they had perforce to seek another home. Going into Hampshire he was struck down by fever, and on recovery was ordered a complete change. Accordingly Southey and his wife took ship for Portugal, and there amid the orange groves spent a most delightful time, being so thoroughly re-established in health that he was able to finish his poem " Thalaba."

Returning once more to England in 1801, he found awaiting him an urgent letter from Coleridge entreating him to come to Greta Hall, Keswick, and eulogizing the beauty of its situation. Yielding to Coleridge's eloquent persuasion, the Southeys joined him there. Southey had not been long there, however, before an important and lucrative post under Government in Ireland was offered him and accepted. But the uncongenial

Bristol's Connection with Literature

nature of the work soon induced him to resign, and accordingly he once more made his home in Bristol. Here he laboured daily at his "History of Portugal" and the "Amadis of Gaul." Here, too, in Bristol, his first child was born.

Its life was but brief, however, and saddened by their loss, the bereaved parents again turned their steps to Greta Hall, finding there a permanent home.

To return to Coleridge, his stay amid the ferny and beautiful combes of the Quantocks was the happiest, most productive, and most interesting period of his whole life.

His greatest poems were inspired during that memorable period. There his masterpiece, "The Rime of the Ancient Mariner," was written. There, too, he was joined by Wordsworth, whom he had first met at Bristol,[1] drawn thither by the wonderful converse of Coleridge, which exercised a charm upon all who came into personal contact with the poet.

The witchery of the sylvan beauty of the Quantocks has been voiced and rendered immortal by these poetic giants. Does not Wordsworth say in his "Prelude," alluding to their rambles and communings over those delightful hills—

> "Upon smooth Quantock's airy ridge we roved
> Unchecked, or loitered 'mid her sylvan combes,
> Thou in bewitching words, with happy heart,
> Didst chaunt the vision of that Ancient Man,
> The bright-eyed Mariner, and rueful woes
> Didst utter of the Lady Christabel. . . ."

---

[1] Professor Knight states they met at the home of John Pinney, 7 Great George Street. It was Pinney who lent Wordsworth the farmhouse at Racedown, Dorset.

Bath and Bristol

Coleridge, too, has summed up their arresting beauty where he speaks of—

> "The many-steepled tract magnificent
> Of hilly fields, and meadows, and the sea,
> With some fair barque, perhaps, whose sails light up
> The slips of smooth clear blue betwixt two isles
>   Of purple shadow."

But the crowning literary glory of this "Oberland of Somerset" is that its exquisite scenic aloofness, away from the busy haunts of men, was the indirect inspiration of the famous volume of poems written by Wordsworth and Coleridge in that memorable year of 1798, known as the *Lyrical Ballads*. This work was not only the splendid culmination of what Chatterton had so brilliantly inaugurated—the romantic revival in English literature —but it has been one of the most remarkable and abiding influences on all succeeding poets.

"The Rime of the Ancient Mariner" and "Lines Written Above Tintern" were alone sufficient to have conferred immortality upon their authors.

It was whilst there that Coleridge wrote that singularly charming note to Cottle respecting Dorothy Wordsworth, which runs as follows:—

"MY DEAR COTTLE,—W—— and his exquisite sister are with me. She is a woman indeed! in mind, I mean, and heart; for her person is such, that if you expected to see a pretty woman, you would think her rather ordinary; if you expected to see an ordinary woman, you would think her pretty! but her manners are simple, ardent, impressive. In every motion her most innocent

Bristol's Connection with Literature

soul outbeams so brightly that who saw would say, 'Guilt was a thing impossible to her. . . .'

"S. T. C."

Wordsworth's sister was equally impressed with Coleridge, for in writing to a friend, she says: "He is a wonderful man. His conversation teems with soul, mind, and spirit." Referring to his eye, she remarked: "It has more of the poet's eye in a wild, frenzy rolling than I ever witnessed."

During Coleridge's stay on the Quantocks he was in constant correspondence with Cottle regarding his own doings and poetic output, and he was delighted, too, with visits from Lamb, Hazlitt, and Southey. It was to Lamb's visit the world owes the inspiration of Coleridge's "This Lime-tree Bower My Prison."

Earlier, we have alluded to Coleridge's habit of reading and borrowing books from the Bristol Library (now removed to College Green). The registers are still most jealously preserved which record the numerous works borrowed and read by Coleridge, Southey, Landor, and Davy, as young men then on the very threshold of their future fame.

It is a record, unique and absorbing in its interest to all literary admirers and students of their works. To the present City Librarian, Mr. E. R. Norris Mathews, the great credit is due of having rescued these priceless registers from the garret to which, strange to relate, they had been ignominiously consigned. The peculiarly interesting feature of the entries is, that in the majority of cases the books were signed for in the autograph of those famous men in the actual registers.

Bath and Bristol

À propos of Coleridge borrowing from this Bristol Library, there is extant in the Art Gallery of the city a pungent and characteristic letter from Nether Stowey concerning the poet's detention of a work in quarto—

"STOWEY, *May* 1797.

"MR. CATCOTT,—I beg your acceptance of the enclosed letters. You must not think lightly of the presents, as they cost me, who am a very poor man, *one shilling and threepence.* For the future all letters to me from the Library must be thus directed :

S. T. Coleridge,
Mr. Cottle, bookseller, High Street, Bristol.

". . . I had had the two volumes *just three weeks.* Our learned and ingenious committee may read thro' two quartos, *i.e. two thousand and four hundred pages of close printed Greek and Latin* in three weeks, for aught I know to the contrary. I pretend to no such intenseness of application or rapidity of genius. . . . I subscribe to your Library, Mr. Catcott, not to read novels, or books of quick reading and easy digestion, but to get books which I cannot get elsewhere, books of massy knowledge, and as I have few books of my own, I read with a commonplace book, so that if I be not allowed a larger period of time for the perusal of such books, I must contrive to get rid of my subscription, which would be a thing perfectly useless, except as far as it gives me the opportunity of reading your little notes and letters.—Yours in Christian fellowship,

"S. T. COLERIDGE."

In May of 1798, Cottle spent a week with Coleridge and the Wordsworths down on the Quantocks, making

Bristol's Connection with Literature

definite arrangements for the publication of the *Lyrical Ballads*, the price of the copyright being fixed at thirty guineas. And on his return to Bristol, Cottle carried with him the MS. of "The Rime of the Ancient Mariner."

This epoch-making collection of poems being ready by midsummer, Wordsworth, accompanied by his sister, set out for Bristol to place them in the hands of Cottle, the travellers visiting on their devious way the Valley of the Wye, which inspired Wordsworth's magnificent poem, "Lines Written Above Tintern Abbey."

The poet has told the world how he wrote it: "No poem of mine was composed under circumstances more pleasant for me to remember than this. I began it on leaving Tintern, after crossing the Wye, and concluded it just as I was entering Bristol in the evening, after a ramble of four or five days with my sister. Not a line of it was altered, and not any part of it written down till I reached Bristol." This justly celebrated poem was committed to paper in Cottle's parlour.

Tennyson, who took the laurel green from him who uttered nothing base, had a profound admiration for Wordsworth's "Tintern Abbey." In Cottle's parlour, too, Coleridge wrote part of his "Religious Musings."

In Bristol the Wordsworths stayed from July to September, for the poet was desirous of being near the printer whilst the *Lyrical Ballads* were passing through the press. It was during their stay that James Tobin, brother of the dramatist, to whom Cottle had shown the MS. of "We are Seven," in the opening lines of which

Bath and Bristol

Wordsworth had "hitched" him in as "dear brother Jim," came and implored the poet to leave it out.

"You must cancel it," he said, "for if published it will make you everlastingly ridiculous."

"Nay," was Wordsworth's calm reply, "that shall take its chance."

Though the edition of the *Lyrical Ballads* consisted of only 500 copies, such was the severity of the reviews and so few the sales, that the largest proportion of the volumes passed into the hands of a London bookseller named Arch. The edition has since become extremely rare and valuable.

Immediately after its publication, according to a pre-arranged plan, Coleridge joined the Wordsworths at Bristol, and were soon *en route* for Germany. In their absence they received the not very cheering report from Mrs. Coleridge, that "the *Lyrical Ballads* are not liked at all by any one."

There were, however, two judges of literature who differed greatly in opinion from the "any," for De Quincey said of them: "I found in these poems 'the ray of a new morning,' an absolute revelation of untrodden worlds teeming with power and beauty as yet unsuspected amongst men." This opinion was shared by Christopher North of *Blackwood's Magazine*. Needless to say, subsequent critics have affirmed their discerning independence of judgment.

After Wordsworth's and Coleridge's return from Germany, the twin poets in the year 1800 were busily planning and bringing out a second edition of the *Lyrical Ballads*, which was to be published by Biggs and Cottle.

Bristol's Connection with Literature

By the end of July some of the poems were sent by Wordsworth to Humphry Davy, desiring him to look over them, "and correcting anything you find amiss in the punctuation, a business in which I am ashamed to say I am no adept."

Later, writing to Biggs on 15th September 1800, Wordsworth says—

"DEAR SIR,—It is my particular request that, if no part of the poem of 'Christabel' is already printed off, the poems which I now send should be inserted before 'Christabel.'

"This I wish to be done even if the press for 'Christabel' be composed. I had no notion that the printing of 'Christabel' would be begun till you received further intelligence from Mr. Coleridge, or I should have sent these poems before.

"The preface shall certainly be sent off in four days at furthest.—I am, dear sir, your most obedient servant,
"W. WORDSWORTH."

At the time of sending the above letters to Bristol Coleridge was constantly with the Wordsworths, and his assistance and advice were rendered to Wordsworth in every possible way in the preparation of this second edition of the *Lyrical Ballads*. Moreover, Coleridge was making drastic alterations and revisions in his own contributions to that work, for example, no fewer than seventy-one to the "Ancient Mariner," in addition to writing an extra stanza; these doing much to improve that wonderful poem.

Towards the end of this year, writing to Coleridge,

Bath and Bristol

Charles Lamb described a solemn call of condolence he had paid, accompanied by George Dyer, to Joseph Cottle, whose brother Amos had just died : " For some time after our entrance, nobody spake till George modestly put in a question, whether 'Alfred' was likely to sell. This was Lethe to Cottle, and his poor face, wet with tears, and his kind eye brightened up in a moment. Now I felt it was my cue to speak. I had to thank him for the present of a magnificent copy, and had promised to send him my remarks — the least thing I could do ; so I ventured to suggest, that I perceived a considerable improvement he had made in his first book since the state in which he had first read it to me. Joseph, who till now had sat with his knees cowering in the fireplace, wheeled about, and with great difficulty of body shifted the same round to the corner of the table where I was sitting, and first stationing one thigh over the other, which is his sedentary mood, and placidly fixing his benevolent face right against mine, waited my observations. . . . I could not say an unkind thing of 'Alfred.' . . . At that moment, I could perceive that Cottle had forgot his brother was so lately become a blessed spirit. In the language of mathematicians, the author was as 9, the brother as 1."

Another Bristol link with Lamb was J. M. Gutch, an extremely able Bristol journalist who achieved a great provincial reputation, so much so that he earned the title of " The Bristol Junius." In the early years of the nineteenth century he was the proprietor of Felix Farley's *Bristol Journal*.

Lamb and he were schoolfellows at Christ's Hospital.

Bristol's Connection with Literature

Writing to Coleridge at the end of 1800, Lamb says: " Soon after I wrote to you last, an offer was made me by Gutch (you must remember him at Christ's ; you saw him, slightly, one day with Thomson at our house) to come and lodge with him at his house in Southampton Buildings, Chancery Lane. This was a most comfortable offer to me, the rooms being at a reasonable rent, and including the use of an old servant, besides being infinitely preferable to ordinary lodgings *in our case*, as you must perceive. As Gutch knew all our story and the perpetual liability to a recurrence in my sister's disorder, probably to the end of her life, I certainly think the offer very generous and friendly. . . . So we are once more settled. . . ."

In regard to Coleridge, for some years after this he was absent from Bristol, but on his return from Malta he again revisited the city in 1807, where his wife and family had preceded him. From Bristol they went to Nether Stowey on a visit to Poole. It was during this visit that De Quincey, who was one of Coleridge's most ardent intellectual admirers, came to the Hotwells, and learning that he was at Poole's posted off to find him, bearing a letter of introduction from Cottle. The particulars of his search and their meeting will be found graphically related in De Quincey's works. How profoundly he was impressed with Coleridge's genius can be measured somewhat by the noble and delicate generosity which, through Cottle, he tendered to the idol of his admiration on learning that he was in financial straits. This was no less than the anonymous gift of £500, which Cottle prudently persuaded him to reduce

Bath and Bristol

to £300. Coleridge's receipt for that amount was as follows :—

"*November* 12*th*, 1807.—Received from Mr. Joseph Cottle, the sum of three hundred pounds, presented to me, through him, by an unknown friend.
                                    "S. T. COLERIDGE.
"Bristol."

Later De Quincey again came to Bristol in 1814, on the occasion of his visit to Hannah More.

De Quincey's mother so greatly admired Hannah More, that she removed to the neighbourhood of Barley Wood to be near her.

In his "Murder Considered as One of the Fine Arts," De Quincey has made classic the Ruscombe murders committed in Bristol in 1764.

Coleridge's final association with Bristol took place in 1813–1814, when he stayed with his old friend, Josiah Wade, at 2 Queen's Square, during which period he delivered a series of lectures at the old White Lion (long since demolished) in Broad Street. This series gave great satisfaction. At this time, too, he became a confirmed victim to the use of opium, so much so, that incredible as it may seem, his consumption of that destructive drug was enormous, amounting to quarts a week. Every effort to wean him from it failed. His departure in September 1814, on a visit to the Morgans at Calne, Wilts, ended this remarkable poet's connection with Bristol.

To return once more to Southey. In the year 1808, being on a visit to Bristol, he met the man of all others

Bristol's Connection with Literature

he most desired to meet, Walter Savage Landor. As Southey says in writing to a friend: "The only man living of whose praise I was ambitious, or whose censure would have humbled me. . . . I have often said before we met, that I would walk forty miles to see him, and having seen him, I would gladly walk fourscore to see him again."

Each admired the inherent nobility of character in the other, and years but cemented their friendship the firmer. Landor, rejoicing at Southey's appointment to the Laureateship, wrote—

> "In happy hour doth he receive
> The laurel, meed of famous bards of yore,
> Which Dryden and diviner Spenser wore. . . ."

In that same year was published Southey's classic *Life of Nelson*, which his friend Humphry Davy declared was "an immortal monument raised by genius to valour."

It was Southey's congenial task to superintend the publication of Landor's famous *Imaginary Conversations*, and it was in his company, too, that Southey visited his native city for the last time in 1836, when he revelled in its glorious Downs and all the old and familiar scenes of his boyhood, welcomed and entertained by his early publisher and friend, Cottle.

To visit the house at Bedminster where his grandmother lived, the church which he attended with his mother fifty years before, his aunt's house in College Green, not forgetting the house where he was born in Wine Street; all this was an unspeakable delight to Southey. Nothing was overlooked that was endeared to his memory by happy bygone years.

Bath and Bristol

There have been many tributes to the nobility of Southey's character, among which Thackeray's generous tribute in his *Four Georges* should not be forgotten. But the finest is written unconsciously by himself in his memorable letter to Cottle acknowledging his deep sense of gratitude for past kindness, wherein he says: "Do you suppose, Cottle, that I have forgotten those true and most essential acts of friendship which you showed me when I stood most in need of them? Your house was my home when I had no other. The very money with which I bought my wedding-ring and paid my marriage-fees, was supplied by you. . . . There does not live that man upon earth whom I remember with more gratitude and more affection. . . ."

Surely such a letter tells us more than many volumes what manner of man was Southey. Apart from Scott, literature has given us few nobler men than the manly, loyal, and tender-hearted Southey.

How he loved Landor may be guaged from the pathetic fact that in the closing hours of his life, when reason had fled from her throne, Southey with almost his latest breath was heard to repeat fondly to himself the name of "Landor, ay Landor."

To the bust of Southey in Bristol Cathedral, executed by his distinguished fellow-citizen E. H. Baily, Landor contributed the sum of £20. But all that was mortal of Southey lies in the beautiful churchyard of Crosthwaite, in the Lake country he knew and loved so well, and Wordsworth was his chief mourner.

Did space permit, much could be said of modern literary giants associated with Bristol, among whom

Bristol's Connection with Literature

must be mentioned Robert Browning, whose father went to school here. Shelley, too, in the years 1815-1816 was visiting Bristol, and in 1829 the world famous Scotch singer, Lady Nairne, was residing at Clifton, where it is thought she wrote her touching ballad, "Farewell to Edinburgh."

Byron also is indirectly connected with Bristol, for Lady Byron was a close and intimate friend of Mary Carpenter, and greatly assisted her by purchasing the fine old Elizabethan mansion known as the Red Lodge for the purpose of her reformatory work. A memorable association is that with Lord Macaulay, seeing that his mother was a Bristolian, and his lifelong acquaintance with Hannah More, who loved to have him with her in his childhood at Barley Wood. It was in 1852 he came to Clifton to recruit his health, and much enjoyed his stay, writing whilst there a portion of his famous *History*.

Nor must we forget that Ruskin spent several weeks at Clifton in his boyhood. In the early years of the nineteenth century, Dean Church was at school here for five years. Kingsley was being educated here at the same period, and in another place is recorded his graphic picture of the Bristol Riots. His friend, Frederick Denison Maurice, at whose feet Kingsley sat as at the feet of a master and declared he was "the most beautiful human soul he had known," had also close associations with Bristol, for he says in one of his letters: "The woods and rocks of Clifton are connected with my earliest thoughts and associations." At Clifton Church he was married.

Bath and Bristol

Henry Hallam, the historian, had close ties with Bristol, for his father was Dean of its Cathedral. And one of the most inspiring personalities of the nineteenth century, Dr. James Martineau, was educated at Lant Carpenter's School, Great George Street, having for his schoolfellow Sir John Bowring, of diplomatic and hymn-writing fame.

Walter Bagehot, that powerful and original writer, whose *Life* has just been published, also spent his schooldays here. The Right Honourable Augustine Birrell says: "To know Walter Bagehot through his books is one of the good things of life."

Elsewhere we have alluded to Bristol's connection with Defoe's immortal romance, *Robinson Crusoe*, and she also finds a place in that other eighteenth-century classic —Swift's *Gulliver's Travels*; for does not its hero start out on his memorable voyage to Lilliput from the famous port of Bristol?

A gifted fiction writer closely linked with Bristol was Jane Porter, the authoress of the *Scottish Chiefs* and *Thaddeus of Warsaw*. There is a tradition that the world owes to her the creation of the *Waverley Novels*, for Sir Walter Scott being one day in the company of George IV frankly admitted that the former novel was the parent of that immortal series. The Bristol Demosthenes, the famous Robert Hall, is conspicuously alluded to in Lord Lytton's *Caxtons*; and in Robert Louis Stevenson's thrilling masterpiece of fiction, *Treasure Island*, the hero meets the matchless scoundrel John Silver at the Sign of the Spy-Glass on Bristol Quay. Who that has read this pirate story does not fail to remember his

Bristol's Connection with Literature

favourite song, "Fifteen Men on the Dead Man's Chest." Then, too, the review of a Bristolian in *The Times* secured the success of Mrs. Henry Wood's most popular novel, *East Lynne*. Bristol figures prominently in many famous novels of our time, including Sir Conan Doyle's *Micah Clarke* and *Rodney Stone*, Sir Quiller Couch's *The Splendid Spur*, Mason's *Courtship of Morrice Buckler*, and Stanley Weyman's *Chippinge*, dealing with the terrible Bristol Riots.

Nor must we forget Hugh Conway, who had such a phenomenal success with his *Called Back* and *Dark Days*, which brought fame to himself and the late J. W. Arrowsmith, his enterprising publisher; and the interesting local and historical stories for the young of Mrs. Emma Marshall, the writer of *In Colston's Days*, *Bristol Diamonds*, etc.

The quaint and picturesque city of Bristol, indeed, admirably lends itself, by reason of its stirring and eventful past, to tales of old romance.

CHAPTER VIII

ART AND THE DRAMA

By birth or association some of the proudest names in English Art and the Drama are imperishably linked with this famous western metropolis. Among these may be instanced Sir Thomas Lawrence, P.R.A., who was born here at No. 6 Redcross Street, and whose father at one time kept the White Lion in Broad Street, one of the old coaching inns of the city, long since demolished.

William Müller, the great landscape painter, was also a native of Bristol, the son of a former curator of the Bristol Museum. Müller proved himself one of the most original and powerful painters of natural scenery, and was one of the first English artists to visit and paint the gorgeous East. Among his most ardent admirers was the celebrated David Cox, who thought Müller a painter of extraordinary ability, and was profoundly impressed with his methods, and as a practical proof of his admiration purchased several of Müller's pictures for his own pleasure and study—surely the finest tribute of praise from one painter to another. Müller died in 1845 at the early age of thirty-three, due to his contracting a fatal disease by exposure on his sketching tours in the East. The great Turner, too, found subjects for his brush in Bristol, for among other local pictures he painted was

Art and the Drama

"The Old Hotwell House" and "A Rising Squall, Hotwells." He was also on terms of friendship with a tradesman of the city named Narraway, who lived at that time in Broadmead. The renowned Hogarth painted some huge paintings for Redcliffe Church, but they have long since been removed to the Royal West of England Academy.

Among noteworthy artists connected with Bristol, Paul Falconer Poole and Francis Danby deserve special mention. Poole was the son of a small Bristol tradesman, and by sheer force of artistic ability won for himself distinction in the world of art. Poole's greatest work was "Solomon Eagle," the enthusiast of Ainsworth's romance. Two of his greatest successes were "Job" and "Glaucus, Ione, and Nydia," founded on Lytton's *Last Days of Pompeii*. He was an intense admirer of Turner, who he boldly declared was the greatest artist of all time. Poole was a superb colourist, the dominant feature of his work being a tawny gold.

Closely associated with Bristol was his great contemporary, Francis Danby, who had migrated here from his home in Ireland, and arrived so penniless that he was glad to sell two of his sketches for a beggarly eight and sixpence to relieve his immediate necessities.

His best pictures were instinct with true poetic feeling. His magnificent painting, "Sunset at Sea after a Storm," received the great compliment of being purchased by Sir Thomas Lawrence. Not only so, but both Thackeray and Disraeli have eulogized his works. Thackeray said: "One may say of Mr. Danby that he paints morning and evening odes." The eminent marine artist and

Bath and Bristol

depicter of some of England's greatest naval battles, Nicholas Pocock, was a native of Bristol. He was one of the original founders of the Old Water-Colour Society, and refused its presidency.

Examples of his skill are among the art treasures at Hampton Court and Greenwich Hospital. A fine work of his is in the Merchant Venturers' Hall, Bristol—"Earl Rodney's Victory over De Grasse in the West Indies." A famous artist and architect, Edward Blore, did a good deal of sketching in Bristol, and some of the most beautiful illustrations to Seyer's *Memoirs of Bristol* were done by him. He was the designer of many public and private buildings, and having become intimate with Sir Walter Scott, he designed and built Abbotsford for him. For many years he was architect of Westminster Abbey. Through George Godwin, Bristol is linked with the world-famous Whistler. Godwin, who was by birth a Bristolian, was an architect, and designed for Whistler his famous London residence known as The White House.

There exists at Boston, U.S.A., a water-colour of Whistler's bearing this endorsement by Godwin : "This was his (Whistler's) first attempt at water-colour." A year after Godwin's death Whistler married his widow, who proved an excellent helpmate and critic of his work, for her suggestions were always followed by him.

Among numerous artists who have shed lustre on the old city an honoured place must be given to the famous Bristol sculptor, Edward Hodges Baily. He was the son of a Bristol ship-carver, and at sixteen became a pupil of Flaxman, under whom his progress was rapid. Before he was twenty he had carried off a prize given by

Art and the Drama

the Society of Arts. Three years later he had secured the coveted gold medal of the Royal Academy, and fifty guineas. At the very threshold of his career he produced his exquisite statue of "Eve at the Fountain," which is one of Bristol's most prized artistic possessions. This work placed him at a bound in the front rank of British sculptors. Among statues he executed during his career were Sir Robert Peel, Earl Grey, and the colossal figure of Nelson, which is eighteen feet high, that crowns the column in Trafalgar Square, London.

A name imperishably associated with Bristol art is that of Richard Champion, of Bristol china fame, who brought ceramic art to a marvellous degree of perfection in his manufactory here. So much so that Owen, in his *Two Centuries of Ceramic Art in Bristol*, states that his productions, had the works been adequately supported, might have successfully rivalled the famous factories of Sèvres and Dresden.

Some of the most exquisite examples of his skill, which for purity of material and splendour of ornamentation have never been surpassed, were presented to Mrs. Burke, wife of the great statesman and orator who represented Bristol from 1774 to 1780. As late as last year (1913) a teapot, sugar basin, cream jug, and two cups of the Burke service fetched over fourteen hundred guineas at Christie's. A magnificent oval plaque, with the arms of Burke and Nugent, costing its late owner, Francis Fry of Bristol, over a hundred pounds, is now in the British Museum. Champion's claim to being the manufacturer of *real* china was strikingly sustained in the fire at the Alexandra Palace, London, in 1873, when

Bath and Bristol

several thousand specimens of English ceramics, made at the famous factories of Bow, Worcester, and Chelsea, were reduced to a molten mass, but the Bristol china passed almost unscathed through the fiery ordeal. Connected with the Bristol china works was the celebrated Henry Bone, whose remarkable achievements in enamel painting have secured for him the proud appellation of "the Prince of Enamellers," for it is doubtful whether his skill in that direction has ever been surpassed. After the closing of Champion's works he removed to London, where, after exhibiting at the Royal Academy, success followed on success, and he subsequently became enamel painter to George III, George IV, and William IV. In 1811 he was elected Royal Academician, and produced his masterpiece, "Bacchus and Ariadne," after Titian. It created a sensation in the art world, and thousands of people thronged to his house to inspect it. He died in 1834, and his bust was carved by Chantrey.

At one period, and that well within living memory, Bristol was an art Mecca of European reputation, for the truly magnificent collection of old masters at Leigh Court, the seat of the Miles family, would have graced the palace of an emperor. Alas! it is now a case of Ichabod, the glory hath departed, for that unrivalled private collection was sold at Christie's in July 1884. Fortunately, Bristol still possesses a few masterpieces that no money can buy, chiefly housed in her Council House. Among these is the magnificent portrait of the Earl of Pembroke by the great Vandyke.

In the civic accounts for Bristol dated 1627 is the following note: "Paid the picture-maker for drawing

Art and the Drama

the Earl of Pembroke, £3, 13s. 4d." Many thousands would be nearer its value to-day. Indeed tradition, no doubt with some real foundation of truth, avers that the family once offered to purchase the portrait by giving as many sovereigns as would cover its surface. Whereupon the then City Chamberlain replied, on behalf of the Corporation, that if the family would stand the sovereigns *edgeways* they would be prepared to consider the offer—surely a striking illustration that Bristol sleeps with one eye open. Within the same building will be found Gainsborough's portrait of Lord Clare, Lawrence's portrait of the Duke of Portland, and Edmund Burke, by Sir Joshua Reynolds.

In regard to Bristol's splendid Art Gallery, the gift of the late Lord Winterstoke (Sir W. H. Wills), though not a decade old, yet it has already a very fine collection of paintings on exhibit there. Especially to be noted is the extremely interesting " Sharples Collection " of pastels. This collection of portraits is of unique interest, as it includes the first four Presidents of the United States, the one of Washington being very lifelike, also Alexander Hamilton. Science, too, is represented by Herschell, Priestley, Sir Humphry Davy, Dr. Thomas Beddoes, Dr. Erasmus Darwin, and Sir Joseph Banks.

In addition to the Civic Art Gallery for fostering a love of art, Bristol is fortunate, too, in possessing the Royal West of England Academy, an extremely fine building opposite the Victoria Rooms, for the encouragement of West of England art, recently reconstructed and enlarged, chiefly through the generosity of its president, Miss Stancomb Wills. Nor must we forget

Bath and Bristol

that very vigorous society of artists known as the Bristol Savage Club, whose delightful wigwam is situated at Brandon Steep, on the premises of that public-spirited and large-hearted citizen, Alderman J. Fuller Eberle, Chairman of the Museum and Art Gallery Committee.

For centuries the sister art of the drama has been well represented in Bristol, for many of the brightest stars in the dramatic firmament, including the illustrious Sarah Siddons, have appeared in sock and buskin at one or other of Bristol's theatres. Whilst it must be regretfully admitted that there is no actual proof that all mankind's epitome, Shakespeare, acted here, yet presumptive evidence that he may have done so is found in the fact that his company visited Bristol in the year 1597, vouched for by the eminent Shakesperian authority, Halliwell-Phillipps.

Though David Garrick never acted in Bristol, he did it the honour of inspecting the King Street Theatre when being erected in 1764, and was so pleased with it that he pronounced it to be " the most complete of its dimensions in Europe." Not only so, but what is more, he wrote the prologue and the epilogue to the first play put on the boards there, namely, *The Conscious Lovers*, with which it opened on 30th May 1766—

> " From Shakespeare's golden mines we'll fetch the ore,
> And land his riches on this happy shore!
> For we, theatric merchants, never quit
> This boundless store of universal wit.
> And we in vain shall richly laden come,
> Unless deep water brings us safely home;
> Unless your favour in full tides shall flow,
> Ship, crew, and cargo to the bottom go! "

Art and the Drama

But Garrick had a far closer association with Bristol, for one of his dearest friends was Hannah More, whose play of *Percy* he brought out and made a triumphant success. À propos of which he wrote her as follows when she was writing it :—

"HAMPTON (LONDON),
20th August, circa 1776.

"We sincerely hope and believe, dear Nine" (in allusion to her personifying the Muses nine) "that you were woefully disappointed at our not peeping in at you at Bristol—you would be a very hard-hearted creature if you were not—so say no more, Madame Hannah, upon that subject. We felt it as well as your ladyship and pathetic sisters. May I take the liberty to say that I don't think you were in your most acute and best feeling when you wrote your third act. I am not at all satisfied with it ; it is the weakest of the four, and raises much expectation from the circumstances, that a great deal more must be done to content your spectators and readers. I am rather vexed that nothing more is produced by that meeting which is the groundwork of the tragedy, and from which so much will be required, because such an alarm is given to the heart and mind.

"I have been in so much company, and have so little time to study your matter, that I can say no more at present. I'll at my return from Brighthelmstone" (Brighton) "pore upon it, and give my thoughts more fully upon the business. Till then rest you quiet and be assured that I am your sincere friend, though at times more bold than welcome.

"My wife sends her love to you all. She has not yet seen your third and fourth" (Acts), "nor do I yet know whether she may be trusted with it [sic].—I am, dear Nine, ever sincerely yours, D. GARRICK.

Bath and Bristol

"You have not sent us what you reprinted about me in your Bristol paper."

It was to Hannah More he presented the casket made from Shakespeare's mulberry tree at Stratford (now in the Bristol Art Gallery) and bearing this inscription on a silver plate—

> "I kissed the shrine where Shakespeare's ashes lay,
> And bore this relic of the bard away."

The very shoe-buckles Garrick wore on his last appearance he presented to her. So keenly did Hannah More feel his death that it affected the whole course of her life, and indirectly induced her to embark on those philanthropic labours in the Mendips which have made her name a household word there.

Closely associated with Bristol, too, was the illustrious Sarah Siddons, for she was the friend of Hannah More and Sir Thomas Lawrence. Here at the King Street Theatre she was constantly acting in the closing years of the eighteenth century and the beginning of the nineteenth. Her salary, it has been stated, was no more than £3 per week! Lawrence was so intimately acquainted with her and her daughters, that had he acted more manly and honourably in his attentions to the latter he should have been her son-in-law. Despite this, however, Sarah Siddons never wavered in her friendship towards him, for on one occasion she said to her brother Charles Kemble, "Charles, when I die, I wish to be carried to the grave by you and Lawrence." When Lawrence heard of this he threw down his pencil, clasped his hands,

Art and the Drama

and with eyes full of tears exclaimed, "Good God! did she say that?"

He painted her more than once, and his portraiture gives us a fine representation of her majestic personality.

The "Shylock" of eighteenth-century dramatic art, Charles Macklin, the friend of Garrick, appeared in Bristol for the first time in 1717, and for nearly twenty years after he was associated with the Bristol stage. So marvellously did he act the part of the famous Jew in the *Merchant of Venice*, that it is related that Pope on one occasion was so struck with his impersonation that he said—

> "This *is* the Jew
> That Shakespeare drew."

Macklin's features were the reverse of prepossessing, and on some one remarking to his famous contemporary, Quin, on the lines of Macklin's face, he was cut short with, "Lines of his face, sir? You mean cordage."

Not only was Macklin famous as an actor, but he was a skilful writer of plays, his *Man of the World* being considered one of the best of eighteenth-century plays.

To Bristol in 1728 came the celebrated John Gay, to superintend the performance of his famous play, *The Beggar's Opera*. Here it was performed no less than fifty times.

A celebrated actor closely associated with Bristol at this period was William Powell. He was in the cast of the first play performed at the Old Theatre, and for three years played there with great success, and ultimately became one of the finest actors of his time. This was due,

Bath and Bristol

first, to his own remarkable talents, and, secondly, to the generous assistance of Garrick, to whom Powell on one occasion wrote : " You, sir, have put within my view the prospect of future happiness for me, my wife, and little infants, who are daily taught to bless your name as the best of friends."

Powell was so extremely popular in Bristol that he was the chief topic of conversation at the taverns and coffee-houses ; in fact, the rage. Any one who had failed to see Powell was considered wanting in taste.

Chatterton has paid eloquent tribute to him in the following lines :—

> "What language, Powell ! can thy merits tell,
> By Nature formed in every path t' excel,
> To strike the feeling soul with magic skill,
> When every passion bends beneath thy will?"

So great was the respect of the citizens towards him, that when seized with his fatal illness, the magistrates ordered chains to be thrown across King Street whilst he was dying, to prevent carriages disturbing him. An affecting anecdote is told of this sad event. On the night of his death, Powell's great friend, Holland, was playing the part of Richard III, and had repeated the line, " All of us have cause to wail the dimming of our shining star ! " when a gentleman suddenly entered the theatre and exclaimed, " Mr. Powell is dead ! " On hearing which, Holland reeled to the wings as though shot, stammered, and came forward, and in a vain effort to apologize, burst into uncontrollable tears. Powell was interred in the Cathedral, and on a marble tablet there

Art and the Drama

will be found an epitaph to his memory, written by George Coleman.

John Hippisley, one of the most famous comedians of his time, was extremely popular in Bristol, where in 1729 he built a theatre at Jacob's Wells, in which some of the foremost actors and actresses appeared. It opened with the play *Love for Love*, 23rd June 1729. Hippisley's great part was that of Peachum in Gay's *Beggar's Opera*, which he originated, acting it for sixty-three successive nights. His very appearance created roars of laughter, due somewhat to a burn on his face received in youth. He frankly admitted that his "ugly face was a farce." When he told his famous contemporary Quin that he thought of bringing up his son to the stage, Quin at once remarked, "If that is the case, it's high time to *burn* him." Hippisley's Corbaccio in *Volpone* was considered a superb picture of covetousness and deafness.

He died at Jacob's Wells in 1748, and in the epitaph to his memory occurs the following lines :—

> "Here lies John Hip'sley dead in truth,
> Who oft' *in jest* dy'd in his youth;
> If acting well a soul will save,
> His sure a place in Heaven shall have:
> And yet to speak the truth I ween,
> As *great* a scrub as e'er was seen."

Hippisley's daughter, following in her father's footsteps, became an actress, and attained a distinguished place among the actresses of the eighteenth century, ultimately becoming the great rival of Mrs. Clive. She too died at Jacob's Wells. A monument to her memory is in Clifton Church.

Bath and Bristol

In Bristol was born on November 27th, 1758, at the Minster House (long since demolished) adjoining the Cathedral, Bristol's queen of beauty — the altogether lovely but unfortunate actress, Mary Robinson, termed by her admirers the "English Sappho." She was educated at the school kept by Hannah More and her sisters. Married in her sixteenth year, and abandoned by the scoundrel who had wedded her, she went on the stage, and soon became one of the most favourite actresses of her time.

There she by her beauty, whilst playing the part of Perdita, captivated the impressionable heart of the "first gentleman of Europe," Florizel, then in his eighteenth year. Yielding to his ardent and persistent attentions, she was forthwith provided with a splendid establishment by her royal lover. But brief was her reign over such a heart as his, for only a year later, in 1781, his father, George III, employed an agent to obtain the compromising love-letters his son had written her. Later, the King found to his dismay that the Prince had given her a bond of £20,000 on her consenting to quit the stage and become his mistress. This she surrendered to Mr. Fox for an annuity of £500.

Having later married one Colonel Tarleton, she lost the use of her limbs through travelling one winter's night to rescue him from a debtor's prison. Finally, in 1788 she applied herself to literature, and wrote and published about twenty novels and books of poems.

How exceedingly lovely she was is proved from the fact that Gainsborough, Reynolds, and Romney painted her, and that "Rainey-day" Smith counted

Art and the Drama

as one of the seven great events of his life of which he was most proud, the incident of his receiving a kiss as a boy from the beautiful Perdita. She died at Windsor on December 26th, 1800.

Through his mother the famous Prime Minister, George Canning, is associated with Bristol, for after his father's death she went on the stage, and had her ability been equal to her beauty doubtless she would have achieved great success. But despite the help of Garrick she was incapable of sustaining leading rôles, and had therefore to take secondary parts, chiefly in the provinces.

At Bristol, in 1775, her beauty attracted the attention of an actor of repute named Reddish, who was manager of the Old Theatre, and she finally accepted him. Unfortunately, four years after he lost his reason, and at length died in 1785 in an asylum.

Happily for George Canning, his uncle, Stratford Canning, was induced to adopt him, at whose expense he was educated at Winchester and Eton, where he rapidly attained distinction in his studies, particularly for his skill in Latin and English verse. To his undying honour be it recorded that, though by reason of his adoption moving in a far different sphere of life, he never forgot his mother. Even when he had become Premier nothing was allowed to prevent his weekly letter to her, and no false pride kept him from visiting her when opportunity allowed. Finally, when he retired from the office of Secretary of State and became entitled to a pension, he at once gladly had it settled on her.

Among the great actors of the eighteenth century

Bath and Bristol

appearing at this Old Theatre, John Quick and W. J. Dodd were ever welcome. No comedian of his time excelled Quick, who played there many times. He was the favourite actor of George III. So exceedingly droll was he, that he must have been "born to relax the muscles and set mankind a-tittering." He had a personal association with the city, for he married a Bristolian.

A Londoner, writing in 1792 of this theatre, remarked that "it was no uncommon thing to see one hundred carriages at the doors of the house," so great was its reputation as a temple of Thespis.

The writer of the famous play *The Honeymoon*, John Tobin, was a Bristolian. This play became so popular that it held the English stage for twenty years.

Two of the most famous exponents of the dramatic art of the nineteenth century are closely linked with Bristol—W. C. Macready and Sir Henry Irving. Here in 1819 Macready's father became lessee of the Old Theatre, and consequently he was often here playing to the crowded houses that always awaited him. In Bristol he met Miss Atkins, who afterwards became his wife, and here also he married his second wife at St. John's Church, Redland, on April 3rd, 1860.

The frequency of his visits to Bristol, and the deep appreciation of his efforts shown by his admirers here, induced in him a strong reciprocal regard, which was touchingly shown when making his last professional appearance.

This took place on January 18th, 1850, when the play selected was *Henry IV*. In his *Reminiscences* he records:

"As the curtain was falling I stepped forward; the

Art and the Drama

audience, unprepared, gave most fervent greeting. On silence I addressed them, quite overcome by recollections and my own feelings to good old Bristol.

"'Ladies and Gentlemen, I have not waited to-night for the summons with which you have usually honoured me. As this is the last time I shall ever appear on this stage before you, I would beg leave to offer a few parting words, and would wish them to be beyond question the spontaneous tribute of my respect. . . .

"'For a long course of years—indeed from the period of early youth—I have been welcomed by you in my professional capacity with demonstrations of favour so fervent and so constant, that they have in some measure appeared in this nature to partake almost of a personal interest. Under the influence of such an impression, sentiments of deep and strong regard have taken firm root in my mind, and it is, therefore, little else than a natural impulse for me at such a moment to wish to leave you the assurance that, as I have never been insensible to your kindness, so I shall never be forgetful of it. Let me, therefore, at once and for all, tender to you my warmest thanks joined with my regretful adieux, as in my profession as actor I most gratefully and respectfully bid you a last farewell.'"

In tendering these words to his Bristol friends, Macready was quite overcome and was unable to check the tears that silently rolled down his cheeks.

The association of the world-famous Sir Henry Irving with Bristol began in earliest childhood, for he himself has told us how well he remembered being taken at five

Bath and Bristol

years of age to witness the launching of the *Great Britain* by Prince Consort in 1843. Here he went to school, after leaving which he was for a time junior clerk in the employ of a large firm of wholesale grocers. From Bristol he started on his great dramatic career.

As late as June 10th, 1904, a banquet was given in his honour whilst he was paying Bristol a professional visit.

The following lines written by F. E. Weatherley, the famous song-writer, adorned the toast list :—

"To Sir Henry Irving

" Let other hands the laurel bring,
To crown thee on the stage ;
Let other lips thy homage sing,
First actor of our age !
We bring a flower that will outlast
The summer and the snow,
Rosemary—for Remembrance,
That will not let thee go ! "

That Sir Henry was touched by this mark of appreciation by the citizens of Bristol is evident, for in his speech on that occasion, he said : "This is a memorable gathering for me—a gathering which adds another link to the chain of affectionate remembrances binding me to Bristol, your ancient and historic city ; and I want to thank you very simply, but very gratefully, for the proof of a regard which I have prized most highly for many a year."

Since his death a tablet has been placed on the house

Art and the Drama

where he lived with his parents—No. 1 Wellington Place, the corner of Picton Street, Stokes Croft.

Irving sat to Whistler for his portrait in the character of Philip II of Spain. This, for which he paid the artist £100, fetched at the sale of his effects on his decease no less a sum than 4800 guineas.

CHAPTER IX

SCIENCE AND RELIGION

CHIEF among the distinguished labourers in the domain of science associated with Bristol stands Sir Humphry Davy, the chemist and natural philosopher, whose name is imperishably remembered as one of the most daring and inquiring of experimental scientists, a tablet to whose memory was unveiled at 3 Rodney Place, Clifton, by Signor Marconi.

He had come up from Penzance, the place of his birth, at the invitation of Dr. Thomas Beddoes, who had settled in Clifton in the year 1793, having migrated there from Oxford, where he had acquired a high reputation as a chemist.

In 1798, being on the eve of starting his Pneumatic Institution, Davy was invited by him to take over the superintendence of it. Accordingly Davy joined him early in October of that year, and writing to his mother on 11th October, he says—

"Clifton is situated on the top of a hill, commanding a view of Bristol and its neighbourhood, conveniently elevated above the dirt and noise of the city. Here are houses, rocks, woods, town, and country in one small spot; and beneath us the sweetly-flowing Avon, so celebrated by the poets. Indeed, there can hardly be a

Science and Religion

more beautiful spot; it almost rivals Penzance and the beauties of Mount's Bay. Our house is capacious and handsome; my rooms are very large, nice, and convenient; and, above all, I have an excellent laboratory. . . . He (Dr. Beddoes) has given up to me the whole of the business of the Pneumatic Hospital, and has sent to the editor of the *Monthly Magazine* a letter, to be published in November, in which I have the honour to be mentioned in the highest terms. . . ."

Davy, with his vigorous and original mind and with Beddoes' help, soon found an entrance to the very centre of the intellectual and literary life of Bristol, for he was soon on terms of familiar intercourse with Coleridge, Southey, the Wedgwoods, and other notable people of the time.

The Pneumatic Institute was opened in March of 1799, and its object principally was to combat confirmed consumption and other diseases till then considered incurable. To this Institution the world owes to-day the birth of modern anæsthetics, for although Priestley discovered the nitrous oxide gas, it was Beddoes and Davy who by their daring experiments revealed its remarkable properties. À propos of which, writing to his friend Davies Gilbert on 10th April from Dowry Square, Davy says—

"I made a discovery yesterday which proves how necessary it is to repeat experiments. The gaseous oxide of azote is perfectly respirable when pure. I have found a mode of obtaining it pure, and I breathed to-day, in the presence of Dr. Beddoes and some others, sixteen quarts of it for nearly seven minutes. It appears to

Bath and Bristol

support life longer than even oxygen gas, and absolutely intoxicated me. . . ."

The inhaling this nitrous oxide (or "laughing gas") became quite the rage. Among those inhaling it were Coleridge, Southey, Tobin, Priestley (son of its discoverer), and the Wedgwoods.

Mrs. Edgeworth, writing from Clifton, says—

"A young man, a Mr. Davy at Dr. Beddoes', who has applied himself much to chemistry, has made some discoveries of importance, and enthusiastically expects wonders will be performed by the use of certain gases, which inebriate in the most delightful manner, having the oblivious effects of Lethe, and at the same time giving the rapturous sensations of the Nectar of the Gods!"

Southey, too, went into raptures over it, for writing to his brother, he exclaims—

"Oh, Tom! Such gas has Davy discovered, the gaseous oxide! Oh, Tom! I have had some; it makes me laugh and tingle in every toe and finger-tip. Davy has actually invented a new pleasure, for which language has no name. . . . I am sure the air of heaven must be this wonder-working air of delight."

That the original scientific work pursued by Davy at Bristol was being watchfully followed and admired, is proved by a letter he received from Joseph Priestley.

"SIR,—I have read with admiration your excellent publications, and have received much instruction from them. It gives me peculiar satisfaction that, as I am far advanced in life and cannot expect to do much more, I shall leave so able a fellow-labourer of my own country in the great fields of experimental philosophy. . . ."

Science and Religion

Coleridge, even after his removal to the Lake district, regarded Davy as the closest of friends, and writing to him from Keswick, July 25th, 1800, says—

"My dear Davy,—Work hard, and if success do not dance up like the bubbles in the salt (with the spirit-lamp under it)"—alluding to the decomposition of ammonium nitrate which he had seen Davy effect—" may the Devil and his dam take success. . . ."

Referring in a subsequent letter to the joint productions of himself and Wordsworth, he remarks: "I assure you I think very differently of 'Christabel.' I would rather have written 'Ruth' and 'Nature's Lady' than a million such poems." Coleridge had many failings, but, unlike Wordsworth, egotistic pride was not among them.

This fruitful time of Davy's career in Bristol terminated early in the following year, when he was appointed Assistant Lecturer to the Royal Institution, and ultimately became the distinguished President of that august Society and the first chemist of his age.

Linked with Bristol was the eminent Cambridge mathematician, Sir Gabriel Stokes, who was educated at Bristol College, and considered himself deeply indebted to the teaching there of Francis Newman—brother of the Cardinal—who was a man of great charm and erudition.

G. H. K. Thwaites, whose labours have added so much to botanical science, especially in relation to India, was a Bristolian by birth. He was a remarkably keen observer and a skilful microscopist, and was one of the

Bath and Bristol

first pioneers to investigate cryptograms in England. J. T. C. Montagne dedicated to him the algæ genus, *Thwaitesia*. To Watson's *Topographical Botany*, he contributed a list of the following plants within a ten-mile radius of Bristol.

Here, too, lived in the closing years of his life William Lonsdale, a geologist of European fame. His work on the corals received the Wollaston Fund and Medal. In the hierarchy of great geologists he ranks with Murchison and Sedgwick. He was the first to suggest the independent origin of the Old Red Sandstone.

Among distinguished geologists associated with Bristol is Robert Etheridge, F.R.S. From early youth he had lived here, and his interest in natural science was first awakened by his grandfather's collection, formed on the latter's voyages, which incited Etheridge to form one of his own. A course of lectures at the Bristol Institution fostered his bent towards the study of natural objects, and with so much success that he became Lecturer at the Bristol Medical School and Curator of the Bristol Institution. Becoming acquainted with Sir Roderick Murchison, Director-General of the Geological Survey, it proved the turning-point in his life, for Murchison was so struck with his ability and knowledge that he obtained a position for him on the Geological Survey, where Etheridge was brought into close touch with Huxley. Later he became Palæontologist at the British Museum, and in 1880 the Murchison Medal was awarded him. The following year the Geological Society honoured him by its Presidency. A famous scientist closely linked with Bristol is Dr. W. B. Carpenter, physiologist

Science and Religion

and zoologist, brother of Mary Carpenter. He was educated at his father's school. From there he went to London University College and to the Medical School at Edinburgh. Very soon his original researches and scientific papers brought him recognition, for they exhibited a broad and catholic grasp of natural science. Johannes Müller, the famous physiologist of his time, paid a graceful tribute by translating one of Carpenter's papers in his *Archives* for 1840. The work, however, that really gained him a definite position among the scientists of his day was his celebrated *Principles of General and Comparative Physiology*. Honours and appointments soon began to shower upon him, including the Fullerian Chair of Physiology at the Royal Institution; the Swiney Lectureship on Geology at the British Museum; and Examiner in Physiology at London University, of which he became Registrar.

He was keenly interested in Marine Zoology and did much valuable work in that direction, including the *Challanger* expedition. He was a fine microscopist, and his valuable work, *The Microscope and its Revelation*, has passed through many editions; indeed most of his works have become standard authorities. It was he who invented the famous phrase "unconscious cerebration of the brain." He was the recipient of many distinctions during his life, including the Royal Society's Medal and the Lyell Medal of the Geological Society; and in 1872 was President of the British Association. His brother, P. P. Carpenter, also attained no little fame as a conchologist, for the great work of his life was identifying and classifying a vast number of shells collected in California,

Bath and Bristol

weighing fourteen tons. This examination enabled him to add no less than 222 new species to the order of Mollusca. The British Association Report for 1856 devotes 209 pages to their description.

Did space permit, much could be written of those associated with Bristol who have left their mark on the progress of medicinal science and surgery. Two shining names, however, cannot be ignored—William Budd and Richard Bright. The first of these is undoubtedly one of the greatest men in national medical annals. He came to Bristol in 1842, and resided here nearly the whole of his life, during which he became physician to St. Peter's Hospital and the Royal Infirmary. The study that ultimately made him world-famous was that devoted to typhoid fever and kindred infectious diseases. When the cholera plague broke out in Bristol in 1866 it was checked in its ravages and stamped out by adopting the preventive measures advocated by Budd. Whereas in the visitation of 1849, Bristol lost 450 lives, in 1866 the death-roll was only 29. An eloquent tribute to Budd's labours comes from the pen of Tyndall, the famous scientist : "Dr. Budd I hold to have been a man of the highest genius. There was no physician in England who during his lifetime showed anything like the penetration in the interpretation of zymotic disease. For a great number of years he conducted an uphill fight against the whole of his medical colleagues. . . . Over and over again Sir Thomas Watson has spoken to me of William Budd's priceless contributions to medical literature. His doctrines are now everywhere victorious, each succeeding discovery furnishing an illustration of his marvellous

Science and Religion

prescience." He died at Clevedon in 1880 from the effects of overwork.

Scarcely less famous among medical pioneers is Richard Bright, born in Bristol in 1789, the world-famous discoverer of Bright's Disease. He was fortunate in being educated under Doctors Carpenter and Estlin. Ultimately he was appointed on the staff at Guy's Hospital, and there rapidly impressed those associated with him with his tireless skill in the investigation of disease. It was his keen powers of observation which led to his epoch-making discovery relating to the kidneys. It may confidently be affirmed that since Harvey discovered the circulation of the blood there have been no English or even Continental physicians who have by their labours effected such an advance in the knowledge of particular diseases, and also so great a revolution in medical habits of thought and methods of investigating morbid phenomena and tracing the etiology of disease as Dr. Richard Bright.

The city of Bristol, too, has had imperishably associated with her some of the most famous men of our country's religious history. Whilst we have no actual proof that John Wycliff came to Bristol, yet seeing that he was prebend of Aust for twenty-two [1] years and must often have preached in the collegiate church of Westbury-on-Trym, it is highly probable the "morning star" of the Reformation did come here. In any case, John Purvey, his friend and disciple, was here in 1384, and he found the city very sympathetic with his labours,

---

[1] This extremely interesting fact has only just come to light, through the indefatigable researches of Dr. H. J. Wilkins.

Bath and Bristol

and it is thought that at Bristol he finished his great work of revising Wycliffe's translation of the Bible. As no city in England welcomed the dawn of the Reformation more than Bristol, William Tyndale, the illustrious translator of the New Testament, was doubtless received with open arms on his frequent visits to the city. A few short miles away in Gloucestershire, Tyndale was at that time acting as tutor to the children of Sir John Walsh at Little Sodbury. Speaking to one of the priests who opposed his teaching in that neighbourhood, he uttered the never-to-be-forgotten words: "If God spare my life, ere many years I will cause the boy that driveth the plough to know more of the Scriptures than thou dost." In the possession of the Bristol Baptist College is a bibliographical pearl worth anything up to £10,000, no less than an original first edition of Tyndale's New Testament—believed to be the only perfect copy in the whole world. Nearly all the copies were burnt at St. Paul's Cross by order of Bishop Tunstall. This copy escaped, and was originally in the possession of Dr. Andrew Gifford, who bequeathed it with other literary treasures, etc., to the Baptist College. Among these is the actual Concordance used by the immortal dreamer of Bedford, containing his autograph of ownership—"John Bunyan, his Book."

Closely associated with Bristol was honest John Latimer, whose call to abjure the sins of idolatry and to worship the Most High in spirit and in truth, was often heard here. In 1534 he preached in Lent at the Dominican Priory, Rosemary Street (now in the possession of the Society of Friends). Though hid away, being

Science and Religion

surrounded by houses, this group of ancient buildings is one of the most interesting left of bygone Bristol.

When Latimer dauntlessly met his death by the fire and faggot at Oxford he was attired in a gown of Bristol frieze, doubtless red, for "Bristol red" was a famous cloth in the Middle Ages.

A famous Archbishop of the sixteenth century—Tobias Matthew—was born here, on old Bristol Bridge, in 1546. According to Wood, whilst at Oxford he was noted for his great learning, agreeable conversation, and the keenness of his wit. He was also a most eloquent preacher, and having had the happy fortune to preach before Queen Bess, he so pleased her that preferment soon followed.

To him, and Robert Redwood, another local worthy, Bristol is indebted for the foundation of her magnificent Reference Library, whose Grinling Gibbons chimney-piece is one of the finest art treasures of the city.

Another Archbishop associated with Bristol was Thomas Secker of Canterbury, who was Bishop here in 1735. Secker had the honour of crowning George III, and was held in the greatest esteem by the famous Duchess of Marlborough, who left him, against his wish, a handsome legacy. He was the true and noble friend of the greatest churchman who has been associated with Bristol, the illustrious Bishop Butler, the Bacon of Theology, the author of one of the greatest theological works of any age or country—*The Analogy of Religion*. Here he presided over the diocese for twelve years. He had a heart overflowing with Christlike benevolence, for when translated to Durham and being applied to for a subscription, he asked his steward how much money there was in the house. "Five hundred pounds," was the reply, upon which the good Bishop bestowed the whole upon the applicant, saying as he did so, that it was a shame for a bishop to have so much. One of the last literary labours of the Right Hon. W. E. Gladstone was the editing of a new edition of Butler's works; and when forwarding a liberal donation to the Bristol Bishopric Fund he desired it to be "a tribute, however small, of gratitude, as well as admiration, to the illustrious memory of Bishop Butler, whose episcopal career was chiefly passed at Bristol."

The great Tractarian, Dr. Pusey, was also associated with Bristol, for his sermons preached at St. James's and Clifton Churches created quite a sensation; and as evidence of the religious intolerance then existing between the two extremes of the Church of England, the walls of the city were placarded with "No Popery" and "No Puseyism." In fact, feeling was so intense that a large body of police were in attendance to protect him from personal molestation. Pusey's daughters went to school at Clifton, and one of them died there in 1845.

In regard to Nonconformity, Bristol has been its stronghold for hundreds of years, and among its great leaders associated with Bristol was George Fox, the founder of the Society of Friends. He first came to Bristol in 1656, and here he held many of his meetings, and ultimately married the widow of Judge Fell, on October 18th, 1669, a woman of remarkable character. As we have related elsewhere, his famous co-religionist, William Penn, was also very closely associated with Bristol.

MARY-LE-PORT STREET : A BIT OF OLD BRISTOL

Science and Religion

Here, too, laboured and died the prince of pulpit orators, the famous Robert Hall, the most eloquent divine of modern times. Born near Leicester in 1764, he was educated at Bristol Baptist College, and from there passed to Aberdeen, where his bosom friend among the students was Sir James Mackintosh. So fond were they of the classics that they were dubbed by their fellow-students Plato and Herodotus. Subsequently Hall became pastor at Broadmead Chapel, and his oratorical flights there became so remarkable and attracted so widespread attention that men of the first eminence were numbered among his auditors.

The great Pitt was one of his most ardent admirers, and said of Hall's sermon on Napoleon's proposed invasion of England, that it was the "finest words spoken since the days of Demosthenes." John Foster, the famous essayist and Baptist, said of him, "All he does and says is instinct with power." Indeed, the admiration excited by Hall's splendid *Apology for the Freedom of the Press and for General Liberty* has led some to say that it deserves to rank with Milton's *Areopagitica*.

Hall possessed a very scathing wit. A story is told that his famous pulpit contemporary, Edward Irving, much desired that Robert Hall should hear him preach, and after some difficulty it was arranged. On the appointed day, Irving, in view of his auditor, surpassed himself, and at the conclusion of his sermon anxiously awaited the verdict. "Well, sir," said Hall, "you presented a magnificent picture, but you stood too much in front of it yourself."

Bristol is also the city of Whitefield and the world-

Bath and Bristol

famous Wesleys—John and Charles. Whitefield's father was a wine merchant here, and his mother was a native of the city. In 1737, when twenty-two years of age, Whitefield came to Bristol ere his departure for Georgia, to take farewell of his relatives here.

He came with a great reputation as an orator, and several of Bristol's churches were placed at his disposal, among others the Mayor's Chapel, St. Stephen's, and St. Mary Redcliffe. He elected to preach at Redcliffe "to such a congregation as his eyes had never yet seen." So affecting was it that high and low, young and old, burst into such a flood of tears as he had never seen before; and multitudes followed him home weeping.

On his return to England once more, he commenced his marvellous labours at Kingswood for the spiritual uplifting of the brutal and degraded colliers, by preaching on one memorable Saturday at Hanham Mount—the audience on that occasion being little in excess of a hundred and attracted by curiosity to hear him. Next day being Sunday, he preached to crowded congregations in St. Werburgh's and St. Mary Redcliffe. A few days later he was again at Kingswood, and now his eager listeners could be numbered by thousands. That their stubborn hearts were melted by his burning message from his Divine Master was eloquently proved " by seeing the white gutters made by their tears which plentifully ran down their black cheeks as they came out of the coal pits." So wonderful was his ministrations that it was not unusual for him to address twice ten thousand hearers.

It was at the invitation of Whitefield that John and

Science and Religion

Charles Wesley came to Bristol—an association that is one of the city's imperishable glories. John's first appearance here was on March 31st, 1739, and at first he had great difficulty in adopting Whitefield's "strange way of preaching in the fields." The first service Wesley held in Bristol was in Nicholas Street, and his first open-air service brought him a huge audience of about three thousand persons. Calling at Newgate Prison on one occasion, rightly condemned by the noble Howard, the prison reformer, as "white without and foul within," he was told that several of the poor wretches there confined desired speech with him. But an express order had been received from Alderman Becher that they should not be allowed to do so. "I cite Alderman Becher to answer for these souls at the judgment-seat of Christ," was Wesley's solemn protest.

In his famous *Journal*, under date May 9th, 1739, he writes: "We took possession of a piece of ground, near St. James's churchyard, in the Horsefair, where it was designed to build a room, large enough to contain both the societies of Nicholas and Baldwin Streets, and such of their acquaintance as might desire to be present with them, at such time as the Scripture was expounded; and on Saturday, 12th, the first stone was laid, with the voice of prayer and thanksgiving." Such was the humble beginning of a world-wide organization that to-day numbers over 30,000,000 of Methodists throughout the civilized world.

Subsequently there were added to this chapel two rooms for the accommodation of Wesley and his preachers, described by him as "a little room, where I speak to the persons who come to me, and a garret, in which a bed is placed for me." To the credit of the Bristol clergy, Wesley was welcomed at several of the city churches, Temple and Bedminster in particular. Referring to his having preached at old Clifton Church, he says: "Seeing many of the rich at Clifton Church, my heart was pained for them, and was earnestly desirous that some of them might 'enter into the kingdom of heaven.'"

The personal charm of this great soldier of Christ is evidenced by an incident related by Southey as occurring when he was a child. He says: "On running downstairs before him with a beautiful little sister of my own, whose ringlets were floating over her shoulders, he" (Wesley) "overtook us on the landing, when he took my sister in his arms and kissed her. Placing her on her feet again, he then put his hand upon my head and blessed me, and," said Southey, with his eyes full of tears and his voice trembling with emotion, "I feel as though I had the blessing of that good man upon me at the present moment."

So many and frequent were Wesley's visits to Bristol that every part of the city was well known to him. Referring to his followers in Bristol, he says, under date August 4th, 1771: "We had six hundred and fifty communicants at Bristol. In the afternoon I preached in St. James's Barton to a huge multitude, and all was still as night." His final appearance in Bristol was on August 29th, 1790, when he preached in King Square. Dying in London in the eighty-eighth year of his age, among his latest words spoken was the name of Bristol, the city he had served and loved so well.

Science and Religion

Eulogizing his life and labours, the Rt. Hon. Augustine Birrell has said truly : " No man lived nearer the centre than John Wesley, neither Clive, nor Pitt, nor Johnson. You can't cut him out of our national life. No single figure influenced so many minds, no single voice touched so many hearts. No other man did such a life's work for England."

Even still more closely associated with Bristol was his brother, Charles Wesley, the greatest hymn-writer of all time ; for he resided in Charles Street, St. James's Barton, for over twenty years—a tablet marks the house. His world-famous hymn, " Jesus, Lover of my soul," is said to have been inspired by the charming incident of a little bird seeking refuge in his bosom during a storm.

CHAPTER X

CHARITIES

BRISTOL, ever foremost in commerce, has also to her eternal honour been ever foremost in philanthropy, especially so in the care of the aged and the young. For her merchant princes in amassing great wealth have ever had large and generous hearts to succour the distressed, the helpless, and those who have fallen by the wayside of life. First among whom must be mentioned the world-famous philanthropist, Edward Colston, for John Kyrle was not more the "Man of Ross" than Edward Colston was the "Man of Bristol," whose noble deeds of charity have immortalized his memory in the hearts of countless Bristolians the world over. Nowhere in the British Isles, and possibly not in the whole world, is the memory of a great and noble citizen honoured year by year like that of Edward Colston. On 13th November, his birthday, the important Societies founded to do honour to his memory meet to carry on the great work which he so splendidly inaugurated in his lifetime, *i.e.* The Grateful, The Dolphin, The Anchor, and others. This red-letter day of Bristol's civic calendar is marked not only by the flying of flags, ringing of the church bells, feasting and toasting his pious and immortal memory, but what is more important, by generous contributions to carry on

Charities

the work so dear to Colston's large heart. He was born on November 2nd (Old Style), 1636, in Temple Street, and was the son of an eminent merchant, William Colston, who took a very prominent part in civic matters; more especially in the sieges of Bristol. Colston Fort, at the back of the famous Montagu Inn, Kingsdown, perpetuates that interest. Early colonization, too, engrossed his attention, for in 1610 he was closely associated with John Guy, the founder of our oldest colony, Newfoundland, and became its Deputy Governor. For centuries the Colston family were identified with Bristol; as early as 1345 a Thomas Colston possessed property in Temple Street. Educated at Christ's Hospital, of which he later became Governor, Edward Colston, following in his father's footsteps, became an eminent merchant, trading chiefly with the West Indies. His crest, the dolphin, is attributed to the story told that one of his ships springing a leak, a dolphin wedged itself in the hole, and so saved the ship. A man of great wealth and princely munificence, he lived chiefly in London, at his country seat at Mortlake, Surrey, and only occasionally visited Bristol, though it ever had a foremost place in his thoughts, as his deeds indicate. Under pressure he stood for Parliament, and was successfully returned in 1710 for his native city, but occupied the position only a short time. He was never married, and to those curious on the subject his beautiful reply was: "Every widow is my wife, and her orphans my children." Among the first of his benefactions to Bristol was the splendid almshouse with chapel attached, on St. Michael's Hill, built and en-

Bath and Bristol

dowed to the memory of his father in 1691, for the "abiding place" of twenty-four aged persons (twelve of each sex).

The Merchant Venturers' Almshouse in King Street, for sailors and their widows, also owes much to his generosity; but his most famous Bristol benefaction is undoubtedly Colston's School—now at Stapleton, but some fifty years ago standing on the site of Colston Hall. This school owes its origin to the refusal by the Corporation of his offer to enlarge Queen Elizabeth's Hospital, which was under their management; some of whom were so illiterate that they could not write their own names, and who held "gifts of that nature only a nursery for beggars and sloths, and rather a burthen than a benefit to the place where they are bestowed." He therefore, having acquired the school, put it under the control of the Merchant Venturers' Society. This famous school, originally the mansion of Sir John Yong, who entertained Queen Elizabeth there in 1574, at which was educated Chatterton, "the sleepless soul that perished in his pride," was opened in July 1710, when a special service took place at the Cathedral to mark the event. It provided accommodation for a hundred boys, and cost its donor £40,000. Each boy was provided with "a suit of clothes, cap, band, shirt, stockings, shoes, buckles, and porringer." It is interesting to note that the costume they wore was identical with that worn by the boys of Queen Elizabeth's Hospital to-day. For his boys he must have good air and a court assigned for them to play in; he wished to make them useful citizens, and so would have them "educated in the fear of God and the

Charities

profession of His true religion." Dying in 1721, in his eighty-fifth year, at his seat at Mortlake, Surrey, Colston's honoured remains were brought to Bristol by road in a hearse with six horses, attended by eight horsemen and three mourning coaches, with six horses to each, the funeral cortège taking nearly ten days to reach Bristol. Here, with great state, he was interred at midnight in All Saints' Church, City—the boys of his school and representative citizens meeting the procession at Lawford's Gate. On that eventful day the bells of Bristol tolled continuously for sixteen hours. An effigy after the portrait by Richardson was executed by the famous sculptor Rysbrach and placed over his tomb. A beautiful custom still exists of placing a nosegay of flowers in the bosom of this effigy of Colston every Sunday, an eloquent token that "the ashes of the good and just smell sweet, and blossom in the dust." His recorded benefactions amount to nearly £71,000, besides the sums he gave in secret. Truly it may be said of this "Man of Bristol," that he has left an imperishable incentive to others to "Go thou and do likewise."

Whitson's Red Maids' School, by reason of the quaint old-world attire in which its scholars appear in Bristol's streets, is quite as well known as those of Colston and Queen Elizabeth's Hospital. Alderman John Whitson, its founder, was born at Newland, Gloucestershire, in 1558, and migrated as a lad to Bristol, where he was educated, and in 1570 was bound apprentice to Nicholas Cutt, wine merchant. At the death of his master in 1578 the management of the business was entrusted to Whitson by his widow, who was the only child of

Bath and Bristol

her father and inherited from him a considerable estate. This being the condition of things, we have it on the authority of the famous Wiltshire antiquary, John Aubrey, who was a godson of Whitson, that he (Whitson) " being a handsome young fellow, his mistress one day called him into the wine cellar, and bade him broach the best butt for her. His mistress afterwards married him." "This story will last," says the antiquary, " as long as Bristol is a city."

Under these fortunate conditions Whitson quickly attained a high position in the city, and in course of time, by the strength of his personality and character, became a man of considerable power and influence in Bristol's affairs, being elected no less than five times Member of Parliament for the city. Aubrey also relates that he kept a noble house and did entertain the peers and great persons who came to Bristol, and being interested in field sports he kept his hawks. Nor did he ignore the claims of learning, for we are told he was charitable in breeding up scholars.

His mansion stood on the site of Stuckey's Bank, at the junction of Corn Street and Nicholas Street. Its stately mantelpiece has been happily preserved, and can be seen in the new school recently built for his " maids " at Westbury. Owing to the discreditable conduct of Whitson's heir, he left most of his estate to the city for pious and educational purposes, chief of which was the founding of the Red Maids' School for the accommodation of forty maids of the city, each of which, according to his will, were " to go and be apparelled in red cloth." A curious item in the dietary of these scholars in earlier

Charities

days was that each "maid" had half a pint of beer at breakfast, dinner, and supper.

The foundation of the rival school to Colston's, that of Queen Elizabeth's Hospital (or City School), situated on Brandon Hill, was due to John Carr, son of a distinguished Bristol merchant named William Carr, who had represented Bristol in Parliament. The younger Carr was a soap manufacturer, having factories both at Bristol and London. His knowledge of the latter city made him familiar with Christ's Hospital, and on that school his own here in Bristol was modelled. He voices his wishes in his will as follows :—

"A hospital for bringing up of poor children, orphans, being men children, such as shall be born in the city of Bristol or in any part of my manor, lands, etc., in Congresbury (Somerset), and whose parents are diseased or dead or fallen into decay, and not able to relieve them . . . with such foundation, ordinance, laws and government as the Hospital of Christ Church in London is founded, ordered and governed in every respect. . . ."

In addition to the founder's benefactions, several others have been received for the benefit of the school, not least that from Colston, who in 1698 conveyed to the Governors about one hundred and twenty acres of land in Somerset. The revenue for the support of this splendid school being chiefly derived from agricultural land, its depreciation in recent years has had the regrettable effect of reducing the number of scholars admitted. The name of the school—Queen Elizabeth's Hospital—is due to it having received from Queen Elizabeth a special charter, or letters patent, of foundation in 1590.

Bath and Bristol

Another sixteenth-century benefactor to whom Bristol owes much was the famous preacher and Church dignitary—Dr. Thomas White, founder of Zion College, London. He was born in Temple parish, Bristol, in the year 1550. Entering Oxford at sixteen, after a course of study there he took Holy Orders, and rapidly forged to the front, and proved himself a preacher of exceptional ability. Preferment followed preferment in rapid succession. Among offices he held at one and the same time were a Canonry of St. Paul's, likewise of St. George's Church, Windsor, and the treasurership of the Church of Salisbury. At his death, by reason of the emoluments of these varied offices in the Church, he died a wealthy man, though it is only just to his memory to say that during his lifetime he was an exceedingly generous-hearted man—proof of which is that he devoted a very large proportion of his income to public and charitable purposes. Thus during his career he did not forget his native city, and in 1613 built his Hospital in Temple Street for the accommodation of six poor men and six poor women, and giving it an endowment. Two years later he further added to its support by giving property in High Street. He also left money for the repair of the roads of Bristol: needless to say, at that early period the science of road-making was unknown, and their state, in wet weather especially, beggars description. In connection with Dr. White's charity there is an annual meeting of the Governors of the charity on St. Thomas's Day — the founder's birthday, when a very curious dinner is provided, popularly known as the "Pease and Pork Dinner." Among the nearly two dozen items

Charities

of which the dinner consists, are two legs of pork, two bellies of pork, two pease puddings, baron of beef (106 lb.), apple tart (99 apples and one quince), and eighteen mince pies. Among those invited to it are the Lord Mayor of Bristol, Town Clerk, and City Treasurer. The menu of this curious dinner, which has been traditionally handed down, has never varied for the last fifty years, and is served on very old pewter dishes. It is gratifying to know that owing to the greatly enhanced value of the property bequeathed by Dr. White, the charity has been considerably extended, and at the present time over thirty persons are inmates. In addition to these benefactions, Oxford University was also richly remembered by him.

Nor in this connection must we forget to mention the famous Thornes of Bristol—Robert and Nicholas—joint founders of the Grammar School. Robert was born here in 1492, and at his father's death was residing in Spain, where he acquired considerable wealth and prestige. In 1515, having returned to Bristol, he was elected Mayor, and later, in 1523, he represented his native city in Parliament. The school with which the name of Thorne is so closely associated was originally housed in St. Bartholomew's, at the bottom of Christmas Steps, the thirteenth-century gateway of which still exists. Its charter from Henry VIII recites that, in addition to the Thornes, there were associated for its promotion Lord La Warr and others.

Robert Thorne did not live long to see any progress made in his school, for he died in 1532. His life had been, however, one of considerable enterprise, for he was one of the earliest of Bristol's merchant adventurers, and when in Spain at Seville was alluded to by the Spanish Ambassador as of "great credence." 'Twas he who urged on Henry VIII the importance of endeavouring to find the North-West Passage. He died a bachelor in London in 1532.

His brother Nicholas resided throughout his life in Bristol, and filled various civic offices, becoming Sheriff, Mayor, and Member of Parliament for the city. He formed one of a deputation from the city in 1535 that waited on King Henry VIII at Thornbury Castle, then the seat of the ill-fated "mirrour of all courtesy"—the Duke of Buckingham—and presented costly gifts to their majesties. He died in 1546.

In regard to the benevolence of Robert Thorne, quaint old Fuller remarks : "I see it matters not what the name be so the nature be good. I confess thorns came in by man's curse, and our Saviour sayeth, 'Do men gather grapes of thorns?' But this our Thorn (God send us many coppices of them) was a blessing to our Nation, and wine and oil may be said to freely flow from him." And again he says : "I have observed some at the church door cast in a sixpence with such ostentation that it rebounded from the bottom of the basin, so that the same piece of silver was alms and the giver's trumpet, whilst others have dropped down five shillings without noise. Our Thorn was of the second sort, doing his charity effectually, but with privacy."

A great benefactor to Bristol, though I fear largely forgotten by the present generation, was Richard Reynolds, the Quaker philanthropist. He was born in

Charities

Bristol in 1735, his father being an iron merchant. Following in his footsteps by adopting the same line of business, and marrying, too, the daughter of a great ironmaster named Abram Darby, he ultimately succeeded to the control of his father-in-law's works, then the most important in England. Under his wise and energetic business management the output of the firm was greatly increased, with the result that Reynolds soon became an exceedingly wealthy man. Settling in Bristol in 1804, he devoted his wealth largely to charity, so much so, that he gave away no less a sum than £10,000 a year. Some idea of the extent of his noble generosity may be gauged from the fact that he employed four almoners to search out and relieve poor and deserving cases.

It has been estimated that he gave away during his lifetime the huge sum of £200,000, exclusive of gifts not mentioned in his private accounts. Dying at Cheltenham, his remains were brought to Bristol and interred in the Friends' burial-ground in the Friars, Rosemary Street. His funeral was a memorable one, for the great crowds who attended were animated largely by feelings of gratitude towards their noble benefactor and friend. A touching story is related concerning him that a poor widow once waited on him to express her thanks for his generosity to her son, and declared she would pray that Heaven's blessings might descend on him, and that when her son grew up she would teach him to thank his benefactor. "No!" was the mild reproof, "we do not thank the clouds for rain, nor the sun for light, but we thank God, who made both the clouds and the sun."

Yet perhaps the most world-famous charity of Bristol

which has appealed to the universal heart of mankind is that of George Müller of Ashley Down, who there built his colossal Homes for the orphans. By faith and prayer they were built, by faith and prayer they are sustained, and the "Narrative of the Lord's Dealings with George Müller" approaches the miraculous, so wonderful have they been. A Prussian by birth, he migrated to England and became pastor of a small flock at Teignmouth, in 1830. Coming up to Bristol two years later, he soon started the great work of his life—the care of the orphans—modelled on the work of his great countryman Francke, at Halle.

He commenced in Wilson Street, St. Paul's, in a very humble way, but the numbers grew so rapidly that further expansion there being out of the question, he made the matter one of Divine guidance, the outcome of which was that he at length obtained land on the breezy heights of Ashley Down, and one after another built those great Homes, to the number of five, at a cost of £115,000, not one penny of which was asked for. In them are housed over two thousand children at an expenditure of nearly £30,000 a year. This great and good man lived to the age of ninety-two, and entire trust in the Almighty was the guiding principle of his life and labours. Dying in 1898, he was buried in Arno's Vale Cemetery, amid a profound and vast demonstration of love and esteem by the citizens of Bristol.

In addition to these noble Bristol charities there are numbers of others of a minor character too numerous to mention. The visitor who explores the ramifications of Bristol's old-world streets and byways will find hidden away many examples of benevolence in the shape of

ST. PETER'S HOSPITAL

Charities

picturesque and ancient almshouses. These are both quaint and interesting, among which may be instanced Burton's Almshouse, Long Row, Thomas Street, founded as far back as the end of the thirteenth century; the Merchant Tailors' Almshouse, Merchant Street; Unitarian Almshouse, Stokes Croft; and the Merchant Venturers' Almshouse, King Street. This last is peculiarly quaint, and forms an asylum for poor storm-tossed mariners and their widows. Over the central portion are these lines—

> "Freed from all storms, the tempest, and the rage
> Of billows, here we spend our age;
> Our weather-beaten vessels here repair,—
> And from the Merchants' kind and generous care,
> Find harbour here; no more we put to sea
> Until we launch into Eternity.
> And lest our widows, whom we leave behind,
> Should want relief, they too a shelter find;
> Thus all our anxious cares and sorrows cease,
> Whilst our kind Guardians turn our toils to ease;
> May they be with an endless Sabbath blest,
> Who have afforded unto us this rest."

The weird fascination of the imaginative tales of Edgar Allan Poe has thrilled numberless readers, but few of them are aware that the extraordinary story of the *Gold Beetle* is founded in all its main incidents on the *Journal of Llewellin Penrose, Seaman*—who was an inmate of this identical almshouse. Whilst begging in Bristol, Penrose had the good fortune to accost Thomas Eagles, the father of "The Sketcher" of *Blackwood*, and his speech and bearing betraying that he had seen better days, Eagles' sympathy was aroused, and after inquiry succeeded in getting him into the Merchants' Almshouse,

Bath and Bristol

where he was comfortably cared for. He proved himself a cultured man, and his conversation about art, literature, and travel was most interesting, so much so that Eagles frequently invited Penrose to dine with him. When at length he died, he left his few personal effects to his benefactor, and among them was his "Journal." This when read to Eagles' family proved intensely interesting. Ultimately he had the MS. copied out, and having induced his artist friends, Nicholas Pocock and Edward Bird, to illustrate it, the work was submitted to John Murray the publisher, who purchased it for £200. The poet Byron was deeply interested in it, and said, " I never read so much of a book at one sitting in my life. He [Penrose] kept me up half the night, and made me dream of him the other half."

In regard to the benevolent race of public-spirited Bristolians, they are not extinct, for well within the last twenty years nearly half a million has been given in benefactions to the city of their birth, chief of which have been the princely sums given by the Wills family for the advancement of higher education and art.

To the noble generosity, too, of a Bristolian, Vincent Stuckey Lean, the city is indebted for its splendid Reference Library in College Green. Not only so, but the cause of suffering humanity has been served by the palatial pile of buildings known as the King Edward Memorial Wing of the Royal Infirmary, due largely to the initiative brain and generosity of Sir George White of Tramways fame.

Altogether, in various charitable ways there is distributed in the city yearly a sum amounting to over £60,000. Thus Bristol is well maintaining the tradition that she is a city of splendid charities.

CHAPTER XI

THE RIOTS

WITHIN living memory one of the most lurid chapters in Bristol's eventful history was enacted in the closing days of the month of October 1831, when owing to the supineness of the civil and military authorities the city was at the mercy of a violent and incendiary mob whose excesses have had no parallel during the past century.

The immediate cause was political, the opposition of Parliament to the Reform Bill; more especially the conduct of Bristol's Recorder, Sir Charles Wetherell, who contemptuously asserted in the House of Commons that the citizens of Bristol were absolutely indifferent to Reform. This statement excited a storm of indignation in the city, and when, shortly after, in the exercise of his judicial functions, he appeared in Bristol in April, his entrance was greeted with very emphatic demonstrations of popular resentment. Matters would have quieted down, however, ere his next official visit had he but observed and taken warning, but unfortunately he committed the glaring indiscretion of again asserting in the House in the following August that "the Reform fever had a good deal abated in Bristol," despite the emphatic denial of the statement by Mr. Protheroe, who represented the city.

Bath and Bristol

Taking their lead, therefore, from the determined opposition of Sir Charles Wetherell to the Reform Bill, the Lords threw it out by a large majority. This lit the fire of revolt in many towns, but in none were the riots attended with such terrible results as at Bristol.

In view of the hostility evinced towards Sir Charles, the local authorities arranged with him to come and open the Autumn Assizes of 1831 in the forenoon, instead of the afternoon, of Saturday, 29th October.

To provide for contingencies special constables were enrolled, and cavalry were quartered in the suburbs, consisting of a troop of the 3rd Dragoons and another of the 14th Hussars. The change of time of Sir Charles Wetherell's arrival, however, leaked out, and on his appearance at Totterdown, where he had driven over from Bath, nearly two thousand persons greeted his appearance with volleys of hisses and groans; these being intensified when he changed from his own carriage to that of the Sheriff's. The procession having started for the city, it was attended by a hostile mob, who vented their wrath in a continued series of yells. At every step the mob's number increased, and on reaching Temple Street, women of the lowest class showed their hostility by throwing mud at the carriage, and shrieking out abuse at the Recorder, whilst vigorously condemning and inciting their male friends to violence. Though naturally disturbed at these unwonted signs of unpopularity, Sir Charles, after reaching the Guildhall and taking his seat in court, courageously rebuked the rabble who surged into the building, and threatened to commit any one disturbing the proceedings.

The Riots

The usual assize preliminaries having been complied with, the court was adjourned till the following Monday, and Sir Charles resumed his journey to the Mansion House in Queen Square, accompanied by a similar aggressive demonstration as had greeted his arrival. At this point the majority of the crowd, having vented their disapproval of the Recorder's conduct, were departing for their homes, and the remainder would doubtless have dispersed had a temperate appeal been made to their better feelings. Unfortunately this latter was not done, but instead, the special constables, mostly young, in their eager desire to show their zeal and to retaliate for the missiles thrown at them during the Recorder's reception, rushed into the crowd and belaboured all and sundry with their staves, ending with carrying off some as prisoners. This course of conduct being continued, the victims and their friends became infuriated at such treatment, and the news having spread abroad, enraged sympathizers were soon attracted to the spot. Reprisals soon followed, for observing the absence of many of the special constables, who having been several hours without food were by permission returning to their homes for refreshment, the mob made a rush on those left on duty and compelled them to beat a retreat. This done, they quickly tore down the railings of the Mansion House and demolished the lower windows with stones and brickbats.

It was in vain the Mayor (Charles Pinney), himself a reformer, accompanied by some of his fellow-magistrates, remonstrated with those assembled to desist, pointing out the serious consequences of their acts of violence and folly, until a shower of missiles obliged them to beat a

Bath and Bristol

retreat. The reading of the Riot Act which followed was greeted with howls of derision, whilst those of the constables who had returned to duty were set upon and mercilessly beaten—one of them being forcibly compelled to throw his own staff through the windows of the Mansion House, whilst another was chased into the Floating Harbour and narrowly escaped with his life.

Encouraged by their success, the mob now seized beams of timber, which they used as battering rams, and a neighbouring wall provided them with destructive weapons for assaulting the Mansion House. In a few minutes the doors and windows on the ground floor were reduced to splinters, and the contents of the rooms demolished.

Soon the kitchens, where a civic feast was in preparation, were invaded, and the joints, fowls, game, and pastry were carried off and devoured; the Mayor and his colleagues being compelled to retreat to the upper rooms, which they did their best to barricade. Faggots and straw were now collected with the diabolical intention of burning them out, but a curious thing prevented it—the inability to procure a light, matches being uninvented.

During this attack, acting on the urgent entreaties of his friends, Sir Charles Wetherell made his escape by means of the roof, and succeeded in getting to a stable in the rear, where he changed clothes with a postilion, and thus disguised easily passed through the crowd who, apprehensive that he would take flight, surrounded the Mansion House, and reached Kingsdown in safety. Later, it is said, he came down into the city to see how affairs were progressing, but finding no signs of abate-

The Riots

ment, he obtained a chaise and left for Newport, which he reached early the following morning.

In the meanwhile the rioters continued their preparations for burning down the Mansion House, but the fortunate arrival of troops in the Square, commanded by Lieutenant-Colonel Brereton, the resident Field Officer of the Bristol recruiting district, frustrated their intentions for a time. The rioters, however, far from being intimidated by the presence of the military, actually greeted them with cheers, and sang "God Save the King!"

Such was the state of affairs when Major Mackworth, aide-de-camp of Lord Hill, the Commander-in-Chief of the forces, reached the Mansion House. He found it filled with special and other constables who had taken refuge there, and who added to the prevailing confusion without being of any service. Both commanders urged on the civic authorities that no firing should be resorted to, as the innocent would certainly suffer. Colonel Brereton, instead of acting with firmness and decision, weakly temporized with the situation by walking his men up and down and shaking hands with the rabble. At length Serjeant Ludlow, the Town Clerk, astonished at his conduct, bluntly asked him what prevented him dispersing the rioters. After more criminal procrastination on the part of Colonel Brereton, about midnight he reluctantly gave the 14th Dragoons orders to charge, but striking only with the flat of their sabres. Though the rioters scattered, many of the ruffians took refuge in the narrow alleys and pelted the soldiers with stones and pieces of iron. The officer in charge thereupon asked for instructions to fire, but the Mayor hesitated, and Colonel

Bath and Bristol

Brereton refused to take the responsibility on his own shoulders. In the meantime a party of the rioters had made a raid on the Council House, and the troop was hurriedly sent off for its protection. A severe conflict ensued, and, exasperated by the missiles hurled at them by the rioters who ensconced themselves in narrow lanes which the cavalry could not enter, some of the soldiers fired, killing an innocent man among the bystanders. The dispersal, however, of the rioters was effected.

Sunday morning dawned and found the rioters again assembling in Queen Square outside the Mansion House, on destruction bent, and, finding that neither soldiers nor special constables were much in evidence, they at once dashed into the premises, and mounting to the upper apartments, threw their contents into the Square, which were either carried off or wantonly destroyed. Previous to this the Mayor and Major Mackworth effected their escape, and made their way without molestation to the Guildhall. Having sacked the upper apartments of the Mansion House, the rioters then raided the wine-cellars, which were reported to be well stocked, and were soon in possession of hundreds of bottles of choice port, sherry, and Madeira wines, which they carried into the Square. A disgusting scene baffling description followed; persons of all ages and of both sexes were seen greedily swallowing the liquors till they became madly intoxicated, yelling, swearing, and singing, till the Square was a perfect saturnalia. The troops once more returned, and the Riot Act was read no less than three times; but to no purpose, for Colonel Brereton still declined to act, in spite of the scene before his eyes,

The Riots

and indeed actually ordered off to Keynsham, some six miles away, the cavalry troop who had protected the Council House, on the flimsy pretext that they were unpopular with the rioters. Their retreat was not effected without bloodshed, for, as they proceeded to their quarters in College Green, they were violently attacked with showers of stones as they ascended St. Augustine's Back, and, firing in self-defence, killed one of their assailants and wounded several others. Returning to the Square, Colonel Brereton committed the egregious folly of begging the rioters to disperse, and telling them, further, that the Hussars had been sent away. A mad thing to do under the circumstances.

A vast mob had now assembled. One portion of it went to the Bridewell, another to the city gaol, which had been erected ten years before at a cost of £100,000; others proceeded to the toll-houses, and others, again, to Lawford's Gate prison. All the buildings were marked out for destruction and were broken into and set on fire. The troops, few in number, tired and badly commanded, rode fruitlessly from one fire to another. The next object of attack was the Bishop's Palace, College Green. At first the rioters who attacked it were few in number, and Jones, the Bishop's butler, bravely withstood them as long as he could; but at length they gained entrance, and were soon busy in their work of destruction, when a party of troops arrived which made them beat a hasty retreat, carrying off what portable plunder they could lay their hands upon. The leader of the troop was invited by the butler to enter, but he replied that his instructions did not allow of his doing so. A few

Bath and Bristol

minutes later he and his troop were recalled to Queen Square, and hardly had they departed ere the rioters, reinforced, again burst into the palace, thoroughly sacking it and clearing out the Bishop's wine-cellars, selling, it is stated, the bottles at a penny or twopence each in College Green. Proceeding from one excess to another, the rioters now determined to burn down the Cathedral, but were bravely resisted by Phillips, the sub-sacrist, and a few public-spirited citizens, chiefly Dissenters, who pluckily assisted him; one of the most energetic of whom told the ruffians that no true Reformer would burn down the people's property; whereupon they desisted and the flames were extinguished.

Meanwhile the liberation of a horde of criminals from the prisons added a still more dangerous element to the already villainous mob of rioters, who only needed such help to be ripe for still further mischief. Accordingly, having already fired the Mansion House, they prepared to fire the adjoining houses. This was systematically done, the occupants being given a brief warning. After destroying the ground-floor windows and forcing the doors, the contents of the rooms were soon at the mercy of the incendiaries; and as most of these dwellings were wainscotted, and the articles contained in them of a very combustible nature, the flames spread with startling rapidity. The sack and destruction of the Custom House were the next flagrant incident of that terrible evening, where, finding a quantity of provisions and liquor, a band of the rioters deliberately sat down to regale themselves, heedless that their more active companions were setting fire to the adjacent rooms. A

The Riots

dreadful fate, therefore, befell many of these carousers, for the flames soon rendered the staircase impassable. Some of the revellers slid from the balcony outside and escaped; others jumped in terror from the windows and were killed on the pavement below; one or two leaped on the portico, the lead roof of which was already in a molten state, and being held fast by the melted metal, were literally roasted to death. A few years after a grim relic was handed round at the British Association meeting, none other than a bone of one of these unfortunates, the cavities of which were filled with the melted lead. Indeed, before midnight of that memorable Sunday the sight presented to the onlooker was that which Charles Kingsley, then a schoolboy at Clifton, has so graphically narrated—

"I was a schoolboy in Clifton up above. I had been hearing of political disturbances, even of riots, of which I understood nothing, and for which I cared nothing. But on one memorable Sunday afternoon I saw an object which was distinctly not political. It was an afternoon of sullen, autumn rain. The fog hung thick over the Docks and lowlands. Glaring through the fog I saw a bright mass of flame, almost like a half-risen sun. That, I was told, was the gate of the new gaol on fire—that the prisoners had been set free. . . . The fog rolled slowly upward. Dark figures, even at that distance, were flitting to and fro across what seemed the mouth of the pit. The flame increased—multiplied—at one point after another; till by ten o'clock that night one seemed to be looking down upon Dante's Inferno, and to hear the multitudinous moan and wail of lost spirits surging to and fro amid that sea of fire. Right behind Brandon Hill—how can I ever forget it?—rose the central mass of fire, till the little mound seemed converted into a volcano. . . . Higher and higher the fog was scorched and shrivelled upward by the fierce heat below, glowing through and through with reflected glare till it arched itself into one vast dome of red-hot iron, fit roof for all the madness down below—and beneath it, miles away, I could see the lovely tower of Dundry shining red—the symbol of the old faith, looking down in stately wonder and sorrow upon the fearful birth-throes of a new age."

So great was the illumination caused by the fires that people could see to read in their gardens at Chepstow.

In Queen Square the most amazing scenes were being inacted : scores of the rioters were rolling about in the last stages of drunkenness, whilst those who were not busy firing the houses were equally busy in securing all the plunder they could lay their hands upon. This they stacked up in the Square and openly sold—a beautiful silver teapot was offered at a shilling, and other valuable articles of furniture at the same rate. How little courage would have sufficed to quell the Riots may be judged from the fact that a solitary porter at one of the warehouses saw a gang of the miscreants attempting to remove the padlock, when he wrested a hammer from one of the men, set his back against the door, and threatened to knock out the brains of any who should come near him. The ruffians at once made off. Similar bravery was shown by a woman-servant in the Square, and by the wife of a publican at Lawford's Gate and her brother in defence of their property.

The Riots

One after another the houses had been set on fire, and by this time (Monday) nearly the whole of the western side of Queen Square had been burnt or was burning, and an attack had just commenced on the corner house of the south side. Providentially, at this moment Major Mackworth with his Dragoons arrived in the nick of time, and, taking in the situation at a glance, saw that if once that house was fired the shipping would be in a blaze and nearly the whole city be inevitably burned. He realized that it was no time to consider or await magistrates' instructions, nor even to defer to his superior officer, Colonel Brereton, who accompanied him. So calling out, "Colonel Brereton, we must instantly charge," and not waiting his reply, he curtly shouted to the Dragoons, "Charge, men, and charge home." This they did with the utmost alacrity, Colonel Brereton, to his credit, charging with great spirit at their head, and the rioters fled in all directions, many of them, however, being cut down, whilst some were driven into the burning houses from which they never returned.

After sabring all they could come at in the Square, the Dragoons collected, re-formed, and then charged down Prince Street adjoining, riding down the miscreants in all directions, about 120 being killed or wounded. Encouraged by their success, a few public-spirited citizens offered their services to Colonel Brereton, who readily accepted them, and seeing the rioters were still plundering two of the unburnt houses on the western side of the Square, they entered and drove them out by main force.

Bath and Bristol

Finding the rioters were likely to resume their work of destruction, and as the Dragoons only numbered twenty-one men, Major Mackworth galloped to Keynsham for the 14th Hussars, who, it will be remembered, were ordered there by Colonel Brereton, and brought them back to the city from which they had been hooted the day before.

On the road they were joined by fourteen of the Bedminster Yeomanry, and the combined forces then charged the rioters vigorously. One section of the troop pursued the Kingswood colliers, who had been very active in the work of destruction; the other executed charges in the city, cutting down all who resisted. With the arrival of more troops under Major Beckwith from Gloucester, the power of the lawless mob, who had created a perfect reign of terror in Bristol, ended. The restoration of order had not come a moment too soon, for all the evil characters of the western counties were flocking into the city to share in its plunder. Four of the ringleaders suffered the capital punishment, and claims against the city for losses incurred amounted to nearly £150,000, though these were on examination compounded for a much less sum.

Colonel Brereton evaded the grave consequences of his conduct by committing suicide.

There is treasured among the civic plate at the Council House an interesting relic of that terrible period —a sixteenth-century silver salver which one of the rioters stole from the Mansion House in Queen Square and, having cut it up into 169 pieces, vainly endeavoured to sell the fragments as old silver. He was, however,

The Riots

apprehended on offering it for sale, and was sent to penal servitude. Such was his audacity that, after being liberated, his first act was to call at the Council House and ask to see the salver, which in the meantime had been cleverly pieced together.

Mr. Stanley Weyman, in his brilliant novel *Chippinge*, has given a stirring and vivid picture of these famous Riots.

INDEX

Abbey, Bath, 4 et seq.
Abbot's lodgings, 66.
Acton, Lord, and Burke's speeches, 21.
Addison, Joseph, 56, 95.
Africa, Bristol's early trading to, 27.
Ainger, Alfred, *Canon*, 68–69.
Aldworth, Ald. Robert, 28, 86.
Aldworth, Thomas, 32.
Alfred, Cottle's, 124.
Allen, Ralph, 3, 9.
Analogy of Religion—Butler's, 159.
"Ancient Mariner," Coleridge's, 117.
Anecdotes—
    Hall, Robert, and Edward Irving, 161.
    Hume, David, and the Bristol merchant, 96.
    Quin and Macklin, 141.
    Reynolds and the widow, 175.
    Silver salver and the rioter, 190.
    Smith, Sydney, and the verger, 68.
    Vandyck's Earl of Pembroke, 136.
    Wesley and Southey, 164.
    Wesley's "Jesus, Lover of my soul," 165.
    Whitson and his mistress, 170.
Anne, Queen of Denmark, 69.
Annual Anthology, 116.
Anstey, Christopher—"New Bath Guide," 10.
Arethusa, saucy, 35.
Arrowsmith, J. W., 131.

Art and the Drama, 132 et seq.
Art Gallery, Civic, 34, 100, 120.
Ashley Down Orphanage, 176.
Aubrey, John, 170.
Augustine, St., Abbey Church of, 63.
Austen, Jane; Bath in her novels, 13.
Avon Gorge, Clifton, 45 et seq.
Avonmouth Docks, 21.
Ayala, Pedro de, 23.

Bagehot, Walter, 130.
Bailey, E. H., 128, 134, 135.
Baker, James, 47.
Ballad, "The Honour of Bristol," 36.
Banks, Sir Joseph, 137.
Baptist College Literary Treasures, 158.
Barrett, William, 102.
Barton, Royal Manor of, 85.
Bath, 1 et seq.
Bath, Roman, 3, 4.
Becher, Ald., and Wesley, 163.
Becket, St. Thomas à, 81.
Beckford, William (Lord Mayor), 56, 107.
Beckford, William, 15, 168.
Beddoes, Dr. Thomas, 60, 61, 137, 150.
Beddoes, T. L., 62.
Bedminster and Southey, 127.
Belgæ and Clifton, 46.
Belzoni, G. B., 90.
Benedictines, Priory of, 86 et seq.
Berkeley family, 66, 71, 79.
Berkeley, Sir Maurice, 82.

Index

Berkeley, Richard, 82.
Berkeley, Robert, 66.
Berkeley, Thomas, Lord, 65.
Birmingham and Coleridge, 115.
Birrell, Rt. Hon. Augustine, 165.
Black, William, 48.
Blore, Edward, 134.
Bone, Henry, 136.
Bowring, Sir John, 130.
Braun's *Theatrum Urbium*, quoted, 77.
Brereton, Lieut.-Col., 183, 184.
Bright, Richard, 156, 157.
Bristol—
   "Bristol red," 159.
   Bristol's connection with literature, 92 et seq.
   Colonists in New England, 30, 31.
   Early maritime importance, 23.
   Fame in the Middle Ages, 19, 20.
   Introductory sketch, 19 et seq.
   Macaulay's eulogy, 19.
   Made a county by Edward III, 21.
   Tobacco trade, 21.
   University, 21.
   Varied industries, 21.
"Bristol diamonds," 55.
Bristol *Oracle Country Advertiser*, 43.
Brittany, Princess Eleanor of, 89.
Broughton, Rev. Thomas, and Handel, 75.
Brunel, I. K., 21, 45.
Buckingham, Duke of, 37, 86, 174.
Budd, William, 156, 157.
Bulls, Pope's—strange use of, 38, 39.
Bunyan's Concordance, 158.
Burgum, Henry, 101.
Burke, Rt. Hon. Edmund, 13, 14, 18, 21, 135, 137.
Burney, Fanny, 13, 55.
Burns, Robert, 98.
Burton, Simon de, and Redcliffe Church, 71.
Burton's Almshouse, 177.

Butler, Joseph, Bishop, 66, 159, 160.
Byron, Lady, 192.
Byron, Lord, 129, 178.

Cabot Tower, 25.
Cabots, the, 23 et seq.
Cadaman, Sir John, 86.
Callowhill, Hannah, 33.
Callowhill, Miles, 86.
Camden, William, 94.
Candelabrum, unique, at Temple Church, 78.
Canning, Elizabeth, 145.
Canning, Rt. Hon. George, 145.
Canterbury, Archbishop of, 89.
Cantilupe, Walter de (Bishop), 89.
Canynge, William, 71, 73, 74.
Carlyle, Thomas, 59.
Carpenter, Mary, 129.
Carpenter, P. P., 155.
Carpenter, W. B., 154, 155.
Carr, John, 171.
Castle, Bristol, 85, 88.
Castle, Egerton and Agnes, 13.
Catcott, Rev. Alexander, 102, 105.
Catcott, George, 101, 120.
Cathedral, Bristol, 63 et seq.
Catherine, Queen, 55.
Champion, Richard, 135, 136.
Charities, Bristol, 166 et seq.
Charles I, 31, 69.
Charters, Bristol, 20.
Chatterton, Thomas, 97 et seq.
Chaucer, Geoffrey, 92, 93.
Chesterfield, Earl of, 16.
"Child of Bristol," 92.
China, Bristol, 135, 136.
Chippinge, 131.
Churches and their associations, 63 et seq.
Clare, Lord, 137.
Clayfield, Michael, 105.
Clevedon and Coleridge, 112.
Clifton Church, 129.
Clifton College, 22.
Clifton, its beauty and associations, 45 et seq.
Clifton's famous houses, 57 et seq.

Index

Coleman, George, 143.
Coleridge, Hartley, 115.
Coleridge, S. T., 76, 108, 109 et seq., 125, 126.
Colston, Edward, 79, 166 et seq.
Colston School, 100.
Colston, Thomas, 167
Colston, William, 32.
Columbus, Christopher, 24.
Conway, Hugh (F. J. Fargus), 67, 131.
Corsairs, Turkish, 90.
Cottle, Amos, 111.
Cottle, Joseph, 109 et seq.
Cowper, William, 98.
Cox, David, 132.
Crabbe, George, 61.
Cranmer, Thomas, Archbishop, 69.

Dagge, Abel, 86.
Dampier, William, 38.
Danby, Francis, 133.
Darby, Abram, 175.
Darwin, Dr. Erasmus, 137.
Davy, Sir Humphry, 62, 119, 123, 137, 150 et seq.
Defoe, Daniel, 38, 55.
Dickens, Charles, 13, 52, 53.
Dodsley, Robert, 11.
Dominican Priory, 158.
Downs, Clifton, 48.
Dramatic associations, 138 et seq.
Draper, Mrs. (Sterne's "Eliza"), 67.
Dryden, John, 6.
Dumaurier, George, 69.
Dutch prisoners at Redcliffe Church, 74.

Eagles, Thomas, 177, 178.
East Lynne, 131.
Eberle, J. Fuller, 138.
Eden, Richard, 26.
Edgeworth, Maria, 51, 60.
Edgeworth, Mrs., 152.
Edgeworth, R. L., 16.
Edward I, King, 69.
Edward III, King, 20.
Edward IV, King, 69.
Edward VII, King, 178.

Elbridge, Giles, 30, 31.
Elbridge, Thomas, 30.
Elizabeth, Queen, 69, 70, 91.
Ellicott, C. J. (Bishop), 68.
Empire-building, 23 et seq.
England, New (U.S.A.), 28.
Epitaphs, quaint, 74, 78, 82.
Etheridge, Robert, 154.
Eugénie, Empress, 60.
Evelina and the Hotwells, 55.
Evelyn, John, 55, 94.

Fargus, F. J., "Hugh Conway," 131.
Felix Farley's Bristol Journal, 101, 124.
Fielding, Henry, 9, 12.
Fiennes, Nathaniel, 85.
"Florizel" (George IV), 144.
Foster, John, 161.
Fowler, John, 93.
Fox, Right Hon. Charles, 60.
Fox, George, 160.
Frampton, Mary, epitaph on, 6.
Freeman, E. A., 83.
Frickers, the sisters, 111.
Friends' Society and William Penn, 33.
Fry, Francis, 135.
Fuller, Thomas, 5, 55, 71.

Gainsborough, Thomas, 17, 137.
Garnett, Richard, 109.
Garrick, David, 6, 138-40.
Gaunt, Maurice D., 82.
Gaunt's Hospital, 79.
Gay, John, 141, 143.
George III, King, 17.
Gifford, Dr. Andrew, 158.
Gladstone, Rt. Hon. W. E., and Bishop Butler, 160.
Glastonbury, Abbots of, 83.
Gloucester, Robert, Earl of, 76, 87, 89.
Godwin, George, 134.
Goldsmith, Oliver, eulogy on Burke, 14.
Gorges, Sir Ferdinando, 29 et seq.
Goulston, Dr. William (Bishop), 95.
Gourney, Robert de, 82.

Index

Gray, Thomas, and Mason's epitaph on his wife, 66.
Great House, St. Augustine's, 31.
Great Western s.s., 21.
Green, Mrs. J. R., 20.
Grocyn, William, 93.
Gulliver's Travels, 130.
Gutch, J. M., and Lamb, 124, 125.
Guy, John, and Newfoundland, 29, 32.

Hagioscope, the, 81.
Hakluyt, Richard, 27, 28, 67.
Hales, John, 18.
Hall, Joseph (Bishop), quoted, 55.
Hall, Robert, 130, 161.
Hallam, Henry, 130.
Hallams, the, 112.
Halliwell-Phillipps, J. O., 138.
Hamilton, Alexander, 137.
Harington, Dr., witty lines of, 6.
Harrisse, Henry, and the Cabots, 26.
Hazlitt, William, 119.
Henbury, Vicar of, 100.
Henry III, King, 89.
Henry VII, King, 24, 69.
Henry VIII, King, 79, 174.
Herschel, Sir John, 18, 137.
Hesketh, Lady, 51, 67.
Hippisley, John, 143.
Hogarth, William, 133.
Holland, Charles, 142.
Hollister, Dennis, 33.
Honeymoon, The, 146.
Hooke, Humphrey, 32.
Hotwells, Clifton, 50, 53 et seq.
Houghton, Lord, 59.
Hour-glass, 91.
Howard, John, quoted, 163.
Hume, David, 95, 96.

Imaginary Conversations, Landor's, 127.
Irving, Sir Henry, 147 et seq.

Jack's Courtship, and the Avon Gorge, 45, 46.
Jacob's Wells, 143.
Jay, John, 23.
Johnson, Dr. Samuel, 14, 86, 97.

Jowett, Benjamin, 59.
Juan Fernandez, island of, 38.
Keats, John, and Chatterton, 97, 98.
Kemble, Charles, 140.
Ken (Bishop), 56.
Kent, Duchess of, 56.
King, John, 82.
King Street Theatre, 138.
Kingsdown and Coleridge, 115.
Kingsley, Charles, 52, 129, 187.
Knowle, Abbot, 65.

Lamb, Charles, 109, 114, 116, 119, 124.
Lambert, John, 100.
Landor, W. S., 11, 38, 61, 119, 127, 128.
Langland, William, 92.
Latimer, Hugh, 158–59.
Latimer, John, 69.
Lawrence, Lord, 58.
Lawrence, Sir Henry, 58.
Lawrence, Sir Thomas, 17, 18, 132, 133, 137, 140.
Lean, Vincent Stuckey, 59, 178.
Lee, Harriet, 61.
Leigh Court, 136.
Leigh woods, and their associations, 47.
Lennox, Lady Sarah, 17, 60.
Library, Bristol, 113, 114.
Lind, Jenny, 59.
Linley, Elizabeth, 14.
Linleys, the, 16.
Lloyd, Charles, 115.
Logan, James, 33.
Lonsdale, William, 154.
Loud, Robert, 85.
Lovell, Robert, 109.
Lyrical Ballads, the, 118, 121.

Macaulay, T. B., Lord, 61, 129.
Mackintosh, Sir James, 161.
Macklin, Charles, 141.
Mackworth, Major, 183, 184, 189, 190.
Macready, W. C., 146, 147.
Maine Historical Society, and Martin Pring, 30.

Index

Malmesbury, William of, quoted, 19.
Malthus, T. R., 7.
Marconi, Guglielmo, 62, 150.
Marlborough, Duchess of, 56, 159.
Marshall, Mrs. Emma, 13, 68.
Martineau, Harriet, 51, 52.
Martineau, Dr. James, and the Carpenters, 67, 130.
Mason, William: his famous epitaph, 66.
Mather, Rev. Richard, 31.
Mathews, E. R. N., 119.
Matthew, Tobias (Archbishop), 159.
Maurice, Rev. F. D., 59, 129.
Mede, William, and Rush Sunday, 76.
Merchant Venturers' Society, 57, 84.
Messiah, The, at cathedral, 69.
Micah Clarke, 131.
Miller, Michael, 96.
Monsieur Beaucaire, 13.
Montagne, J. T. C., 154.
Moore, Thomas, 108.
More, Hannah, 61, 126, 129, 139, 140, 144.
Morocco, early Bristol trading to, 27.
Müller, George, 176.
Müller, W. J., 69, 132.
Murchison, Sir Roderick, 154.
Murray, John, publisher, 178.

Nairne, Lady, 129.
Napier, Sir William, 17.
Nash, Richard (Beau), 7, 8.
Nelson, Horatio, Lord, 16, 127.
Nether Stowey, 115, 120.
"New Bath Guide," Anstey's, 10, 11.
Newfoundland, 24, 32, 33.
Newman, Francis, 153.
New Testament, Tyndale's unique, 158.
Newton, Lady, 86.
Nightingale Valley, Clifton, and Ruskin, 47.
Norfolk, Duke of, at Temple Church, 77.

North, Christopher, 122.
Norton, William, 93.
"Norwich, Three Gentlemen of," 54.

Ortelius, the geographer, at Temple Church, 77.
Owen, Hugh, *Two Centuries of Ceramic Art in Bristol*, 135.
Oxford, Greek first taught at, 93.

Parry, Sir Edward, 18.
Pasqualigo, Lorenzo, 25.
"Pease and Pork Dinner," curious, 172, 173.
Pembroke, Earl of, Vandyck's portrait of, 136.
Penn, William, 33, 34, 160.
Penn, Admiral Sir William, 74.
Penrose, Llewellin, Journal of, 177, 178.
Penzance, corsairs at, 90.
Pepys, Samuel, at Bristol, 94, 95.
Pickwick Papers, 13, 52, 53.
Pierrepont Street memories, 16.
Pilgrim Fathers, 28.
Pinney, Charles (Mayor), 181.
Piozzi, Mrs. *See* Thrale.
Pirate, Scott's, and Bristol, 40.
Pitt, Rt. Hon. William, 15, 161.
Plymouth, New England, 28.
Pneumatic Institution, Hotwells, 150 et seq.
Pocock, Nicholas, 134, 178.
Poe, E. A., 177.
Poole, P. F., 133.
Poole, Thomas, 114.
Pope, Alexander, 9, 96, 141.
Popham, Lord Chief Justice, 29.
Porter, Jane, 130.
Portland, Duke of, 137.
Powell, William, 141, 142.
Poyntz, Sir Robert, 81.
Priestley, Joseph, 152.
Pring, Martin, 28, 29, 30, 84.
Privateering, Bristol, 35 et seq.
Prynne, William, 18.
Purvey, John, 157.
Pusey, E. B., 160.

Index

Quantocks, the, Somerset, 117–119.
Queen Elizabeth's Hospital (City School), 168, 171.
Queensberry, Duchess of, and Beau Nash, 7, 8.
Quick, John, 146.
Quin, James, 143.

Redcliffe Church, St. Mary, 70 et seq.
Red Maids' School, 169, 170.
Reynolds, Sir Joshua, 137.
Reynolds, Richard, 174, 175.
"Richard the Redeless," 92.
Richardson, Samuel, 9.
Riots, Bristol, 179 et seq.
Roberts, Field-Marshal Lord, 60.
Robinson Crusoe, 38.
Robinson, Mary (Perdita), 116, 144.
Rodney Stone, 131.
Rogers, Captain Woodes, 38, 39.
Rosebery, Lord, 21.
Rowley, Thomas, 91.
Rupert, Prince, 85, 91.
Ruskin, John, 47.
Russell, W. Clark, 45.

St. James's Church, 86 et seq.
St. James's Fair, 89, 90.
St. John's Church, 90 et seq.
St. Mark's (Lord Mayor's Chapel), 79 et seq.
St. Mary Redcliffe Church, 70 et seq.
St. Peter's Church, 85–6.
St. Peter's Hospital, 86.
St. Stephen's Church, 83 et seq.
Salley, Miles (Bishop), 80, 82.
Savage Club, Bristol, 138.
Savage, Richard, 86, 97.
Science and Religion, 150 et seq.
Scott, Sir Walter, 17, 104, 108, 130.
Secker, Thomas (Archbishop), 159.
Selkirk, Alexander ("Robinson Crusoe"), 38.
Seyer's *Memoirs of Bristol*, 134.
"Sharples Collection," 137.

Shaw, Captain John, epitaph to, 44.
Shelley, P. B., 98, 129.
Sheridan, Mrs., 18.
Sheridan, R. B., 14.
Shipward, John, 83.
Siddons, Mrs. Sarah, 138.
Sieges of Bristol, 85, 91.
Smalridge, George (Bishop), 95.
Smith, Sir Sidney, 17.
Smith, Rev. Sydney, 61, 67, 68.
Smollett, Tobias, and Bath, 12.
Smyth, Sir Hugh, 32.
Snigge, Sir George, 84.
Southey, Robert, 11, 15, 76, 108 et seq., 119, 128, 152.
Splendid Spur, The, 131.
Stephens, Robert and Henry, 93.
Sterling, John, 59.
Sterne, Laurence, 18.
Stevenson, R. L., 59, 130.
Stokes, Sir Gabriel, 153.
Stokesleigh camp, Clifton, 47.
Stradling, Sir John, 93, 94.
Strange Adventures of a House Boat, 48, 49.
Suspension Bridge, Clifton, 45.
Swinburne, A. C., eulogy on Bath, 2.
Symonds, J. A., 58, 64.

Tarkington, Booth, 13.
Templars, Knights, 76.
Temple Almshouse, 172.
Temple Church, 76 et seq.
Tennyson, Alfred, Lord, 121.
Thackeray, W. M., 128, 133.
Theatrum Urbium, quoted, 77.
Thorne, Nicholas, 174.
Thorne, Robert, 27, 173 et seq.
Thrale, Mrs. (Piozzi), 51, 60.
Thwaites, G. H. K., 153.
"Tintern, Lines Written Above," 118, 121.
Tobacco trade of Bristol, 21.
Tobin, John, 146.
Treasure Island, 40, 130.
Treasure ships captured, 43.
Turner, J. M. W., 132, 133.

Index

Tyndale, William, 64, 158.

Vandyck, Sir Anthony, 136.
Vathek, Beckford's, 16.
Virginia Company, 29.
Virginia, North, 28.

Wade, Josiah, 126.
Waller, Lady Jane, 6.
Walpole, Horace, 10, 102, 103.
Watchman, The, Coleridge's, 113, 114.
Watts-Dunton, Theodore, 108.
"We are Seven," 121.
Weaver's Chapel, Temple Church, 77.
Wedgwood, Thomas, 59.
Wells and Bath, 5.
Wells Cathedral, 91.
Wesley, Charles, 90, 163, 165.
Wesley, John, 56, 69, 79, 162 et seq.
Westbury-on-Trym Church, 157.
Wetherell, Sir Charles, 179 et seq.
Whistler, J. A. M'Neill, 134, 149.
White, Sir George, 178.
White, Gilbert, 56.
White, Dr. Thomas, 172.

Whitefield, George, 75, 161, 162.
Whitelocke, Bulstrode, 55.
Whitson, Ald. John, 28, 169, 170.
Wilkins, Dr. H. J., 157 *note*.
Will, Chatterton's, 106.
Wills family, 178.
Wills, Miss Stancomb, 137.
Winterstoke, Lord (Sir W. H. Wills), 137.
Wolfe, James (General), 17.
Wood, Anthony, 93.
Wood, Mrs. Henry, *East Lynne*, 131.
Woods, architects of Bath, 1.
Wordsworth, Dorothy, 118.
Wordsworth, William, 15, 108, 109, 117 et seq.
Wycestre, William (Botoner), 54, 92.
Wycliff, John, 157.

Yearsley, Ann, 59.
Yeoman and Boucher, 91.
Yong, Sir John, and Queen Elizabeth, 168.
Young, Thomas, 93.

Zion College, 173.